SAVING
CALIFORNIA

Saving California: Solutions to the state's biggest policy problems

Edited by Steven Greenhut
Wendell Cox, Lance Izumi, Dan Kolkey, Joel Kotkin, Adrian Moore, Richard Mersereau,
Pat Nolan, Sally Pipes, Wayne Winegarden

August 2021

ISBN: 978-1-934276-44-0

Book design: Dana Beigel
Photo credits: pages 3, 11, 25, 137 ©Shutterstock; page 43 ©Flickr/Daniel Ramirez;
page 55 ©Flickr/Daniel R. Blume; page 67 ©Flickr/Robert Couse Baker; page 79 ©Flickr/
Mundial Perspectives; page 95 ©Flickr/Paul Sableman; page 109 ©iStockphoto;
page 123 ©Flickr/National Interagency Fire Department; page 149 ©DepositPhotos.

Pacific Research Institute
680 E. Colorado Blvd., Suite 180
Pasadena, CA 91101

Tel: 415-989-0833
Fax: 415-989-2411
www.pacificresearch.org

SAVING CALIFORNIA

Solutions to the state's biggest policy problems

EDITED BY STEVEN GREENHUT

WENDELL COX • LANCE IZUMI • DAN KOLKEY

JOEL KOTKIN • ADRIAN MOORE

RICHARD MERSEREAU • PAT NOLAN

SALLY PIPES • WAYNE WINEGARDEN

CONTENTS

INTRODUCTION: SAVING CALIFORNIA

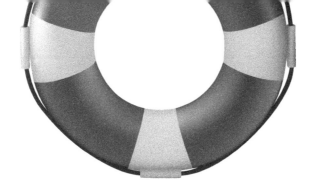

INTRODUCTION
SAVING CALIFORNIA

By Steven Greenhut

*At my feet lay the Great Central Valley of California, level
and flowery, like a lake of pure sunshine, forty or fifty
miles wide, five hundred miles long, one rich furred garden
of yellow Compositae. And from the eastern boundary of
this vast golden flower-bed rose the mighty Sierra, miles in
height, and so gloriously colored and so radiant, it seemed
not clothed with light but wholly composed of it, like the wall
of some celestial city.*
> —*John Muir, naturalist*

One of my best memories of encountering California came in 1998, as I was moving from a small industrial city in Ohio. I crossed the Colorado River, in a packed car with a panting dog and disgruntled cat, and pulled over at a rest stop outside of Needles. The thermometer topped 110 degrees. I noted the "rattlesnake warning" signs posted along the sidewalk. The scorching Mojave Desert is a long way from John Muir's vision of the verdant valley and Sierra Nevada, but I still recall my sense of wonder and thinking, "I'm already in love with this state."

A few weeks earlier, the *Orange County Register*'s editorial page editor Cathy Taylor had offered me a plum job as an editorial writer at the newspaper, which was Freedom Communications' flagship publication. I had been working as an opinion writer at one of the newspaper group's smaller dailies, *The Lima News*, and having a great time tormenting local officials. But I had spent my three years there plotting my escape to Southern California.

My colleagues thought I was nuts. Even 25 years ago, much of the luster had worn off the Golden State. "You would seriously move to *California*?" they'd ask in near disbelief. Quentin Tarantino's *Pulp Fiction* had recently been released, and my Ohio friends really thought that its story of Los Angeles' seedy underbelly – with drug overdoses, assorted sleazebags, rampant violence, and dilapidated strip malls – was all that the state had to offer. I couldn't understand how anyone would stay in a hardscrabble factory town when the lights and palm trees of California were an option.

My family rented a 1940s bungalow in Fullerton, in north Orange County. When we looked for houses in the area – which cost at least three times what they cost in northwest Ohio – my wife broke down in tears. The stucco tract houses, freeways and office towers seemed so alien. Donna couldn't imagine how she'd find her way around the sprawling metropolis, but I told her to pretend that nothing existed outside of Fullerton. Within weeks, she adapted. She soon was venturing out on the 57, 5 and 22 freeways. It wasn't love at first sight for her, but she grew to love the place, too.

I've never lost my sense of wonder at all that is California. As environmentalist author Edward Abbey once wrote, "There is science, logic, reason; there is thought verified by experience. And then there is California." A lot of what makes California what it is – and what it had always been, in perception or reality – defies logic and reason. I've since moved to the Sacramento area and have traveled to every corner of the state, visiting every one of its 58 counties. On a recent trip back from the lush Pacific Northwest, I was nevertheless thrilled to cross into Siskiyou County and into the Sacramento Valley, where the Sierras towered in the distance like Muir's celestial city.

As a political writer, I've spent most of my career documenting the disastrous public-policy choices made by California's elected officials. That sometimes causes readers to lump me in with the vocal group of mostly non-Californian conservatives, writing from Washington, D.C., or New York City, who disdain the state. "(A)s they portray it, the Golden State is a Banana Republic," wrote Max Taves, in the *Sacramento Bee*. "It's a violent, poverty-stricken homeless infernal dystopia overrun by MS-13 and misled by incompetent criminal-coddling politicians whose radical, immigrant-loving, left-wing agenda is horrible for businesses, which are leaving the state in droves."

In my *Orange County Register* rebuttal, I argued that many of us – in fact, most of the California critics of the state's more recent political tilt who I know – love California and want to save it from a new breed of politicians that views it mainly as a laboratory for progressive experiments. We don't expect – nor want – California to be governed as if it's Alabama or North Dakota but believe that current officials misunderstand what has always drawn people here. Sure, California's politics will never mirror mine – at least not in my lifetime. Progressivism is to some degree baked into our DNA. One need only think about Gov. Hiram Johnson (father of the initiative, recall and referendum) and Upton Sinclair (author and socialist governor candidate) to understand that.

But California has also always been a land of opportunity, even if the grandiose Gold Rush and post-war dreams of effortless wealth have been mostly fantasy. My wish is to rekindle some of that excitement and energy that has always brought people to California. During the Gold Rush, California's population exploded by 310 percent in 10 years. The 49ers came from across the globe seeking wealth and new lives. When I moved to California in 1998, the population was just shy of 33 million. It has since grown to nearly 40 million – but it can't quite get there. The Department of Finance reported this year an actual loss in population for the first time in more than a century.

In 1998, I covered the story of a business that was moving out of state from its location in an industrial park in Vernon, just south of downtown Los Angeles. Other business owners who attended the press conference eagerly compared notes about the best states to move. That saddened me. Even then, my acquaintances often talked about where they'd be going – although not as much as they do now. A neighbor from Fullerton now runs a bustling real-estate business in Texas, where she finds homes for literal busloads of Californians heading to the Dallas area.

During the 2003 gubernatorial recall debate, Tom McClintock, now a U.S. congressman who represents Placer County, bemoaned the state of public policy that made the Arizona and Nevada deserts seem like a better place to raise a family than California. The recall succeeded – but didn't change the state's political trajectory. As of this writing, another recall election is headed for the ballot. Even if it succeeds, it will be only a year before California holds a regularly scheduled governor's election. There may be good reasons for a recall but reinvigorating our state will take more than political activism.

This book takes no position on such matters, but it is focused on policy changes that could help restore some of California's lost luster – regardless of what politician runs our massive state government apparatus. It's not about political campaigns.

The authors are all current or former Californians, people with deep expertise in their respective policy areas. Although their chapters include a fair share of criticism of current policy directions – how could they not? – they propose real-world policy changes that could push the state onto a better track. I'm not naïve. I don't expect the current slate of politicians to abandon their special-interest-group commitments, have a Road to Damascus moment and embrace the kind of policies that will once again make the Golden State a destination for those who seek out opportunity. That said, many of the ideas and thought experiments proposed within these pages are realistic reforms that advance the stated goals even of the most progressive legislators, such as bettering the environment and helping the poor.

For instance, Joel Kotkin points to the need for reform of the California Environmental Quality Act, the landmark 1970 environmental law that has impeded the construction of housing and other projects. Virtually all of the state's Democratic leaders have, at one time or another, paid lip service to that idea. Wendell Cox proposes a novel idea for boosting housing affordability, starting in California's inland regions. Wayne Winegarden's proposals for addressing the homeless crisis are non-ideological, cost-effective, and humane. Adrian Moore lists a variety of straightforward infrastructure strategies, the likes of which have been embraced in other states. My chapter on water points to time-proven methods for boosting water abundance, although many of these proposals require that state officials plan ahead rather than merely react to the latest drought.

Until recently, California Democrats have largely been supportive of charter schools – and Lance Izumi points to a way back toward that consensus, with an eye toward boosting the prospects of disadvantaged communities. Pat Nolan points to the growing crime wave but offers reform-minded solutions that would create a less brutal criminal-justice system.

Richard Mersereau spent his career within the bowels of the state Capitol and his budget reforms would set the state on a more sustainable course. Dan Kolkey's in-depth look at wildfire policy would help – not hinder – California's commitment to battling climate change. And Sally Pipes offers healthcare solutions that could help provide Californians with the care they need. It's a far cry from the push by progressives for single-payer solutions – something that seems more about political posturing than making real-world improvements.

Every one of this book's authors propose good-government policies that politicians from either party could easily adopt without forcing them to depart from their overall political objectives. Again, this book is about identifying the state's problems and offering a path toward better solutions. It's not a call to political action, nor is it in any way partisan.

Even though every idea faces political hurdles, I still believe it's important to build a framework for good policymaking that's available when the time is right. I think back to the mid-2000s, when I was part of a group of writers, lawmakers and activists who had spotlighted the ill effects of California's redevelopment agencies. These were locally controlled state agencies that floated debt, subsidized private developments, and used eminent domain to grab land on behalf of developers. Redevelopment got its start in the 1940s, as a means to combat urban blight. But it morphed into a system whereby city councils used their power to boost sales-tax revenues. It distorted development decisions, undermined property rights and helped lead to our current housing shortages (because cities preferred approving tax-rich retail complexes to apartments and housing tracts).

The battle seemed hopeless given the power of the groups, such as the California League of Cities and the California Redevelopment Association, that supported the system's various subsidies and power grabs. Then, a crisis unfolded. California faced growing budget deficits and then-Gov. Jerry Brown needed to plug a gaping budget hole. Because these agencies diverted a large portion of property taxes from traditional public services (and the state had to backfill the missing dollars), Brown decided to shutter the agencies. Like so many of the reform ideas discussed in this book, the intellectual framework for redevelopment reform had already been laid by lawmakers such as former GOP Assemblyman Chris Norby of Orange County and former Independent Sen. Quentin Kopp of San Francisco. Brown was able to turn to a once-improbable idea to solve another problem because the blueprint had already been printed.

Likewise, this book highlights the state's core challenges – business climate, housing, homelessness, infrastructure, water policy, education, crime, budgets and debt, wildfires, and healthcare – and offers some solutions that are available whenever the timing is right to consider them, or when a crisis unfolds that mandates some out-of-the-box thinking. We're creating a framework for reform, whether or not any policymakers now are clamoring for such ideas.

Although the California Dream is in the eye of the beholder, I do believe we can recreate a consensus that's committed to rebuilding and re-energizing California – not as a world of pipedreams (although a little dreaming has its place), but as a special state whose beauty and opportunities can still draw people like me from other places.

CHAPTER ONE: GETTING BACK TO BUSINESS

CHAPTER ONE
GETTING BACK TO BUSINESS

By Joel Kotkin

From the Beginning, California promised much. While yet barely a name on the map, it entered American awareness as a symbol of renewal. It was a final frontier: of geography and of expectation.

—Kevin Starr,
Americans and the
California Dream: 1850-1915

In the eyes of both those who live here, and those who come to observe, California has long stood out as the beacon for a better future. Laura Tyson and Lenny Mendonca still see California as the home of "a new progressive era," the exemplar of social justice.[1] Progressive writers Peter Leyden and Ruy Teixeira wrote in 2018 in *Medium*, that California is the future of American politics.[2] An ecstatic account in the *Los Angeles Times* suggests that President Joe Biden's goal is to "make America California again."[3]

Yet if they looked beyond the rhetoric, many traditional liberals might wonder if the California model is more of a cautionary tale than a roadmap to a better future in the digital age. Indeed, the on-the-ground reality is increasingly more Dickensian than utopian. Rather than a state that epitomizes the middle-class dreamscape, California increasingly presents the prototype of a new feudalism fused oddly with a new, fundamentally socially regressive progressive model.

California now suffers the highest cost-adjusted poverty rate in the country, and the widest gap between middle- and upper-middle income earners.[4] It also has one of the nation's highest Gini ratios, which measures the inequality of wealth distribution from the richest to poorest residents – and the disparity is growing. As the working class and poor decline, while the super-rich have grown in numbers, the state now suffers a level of inequality worse than Mexico.[5]

The Evolution of the California Economy

Progressives can point with pride to their role in building the old California economy. Under Pat Brown and earlier governors, the state invested heavily in infrastructure and education, while its politicians worked overtime to attract investment. Even Gov. Jerry Brown in his first term embraced the notion that Californians would benefit from its central position on the Pacific Rim as well as its dominance of technology and space exploration.

Until the past decade, the technology industry was part of a remarkably diverse economy, resting on an array of industries that spanned the gamut from agriculture and oil to aerospace and finance, software and basic manufacturing. The broad range of opportunities – plus the unmatched beauty and mild climate – lured millions of people from around the world, from literal "rocket scientists" to impoverished *campesinos*.

In the process, California developed a large and increasingly diverse middle class. "The California Century," notes Ethan Rarick, biographer of Jerry Brown's father Pat Brown, provided "the template of American Life." There was an 'American Dream' across the nation, he noted, "but here we had the 'California Dream.'" [6]

As recently as the 1996-2006 period, notes economist David Friedman, the state created a vast array of jobs spread across job types, geographies, and incomes. But after the Great Recession, the state's economy became more narrowly focused and geographically constrained – centering almost exclusively around the tech-driven San Francisco Bay Area economy.[7] Yet even this boom seems to be fading as major Bay Area firms such as Hewlett Packard and Oracle and many smaller tech firms head for more business-friendly climes.

In the last few years, California's regulatory and tax regime has driven a host of companies that once provided middle-class and solid blue-collar jobs to the exits. These include long-term stalwarts as Occidental Petroleum, Jacob's Engineering, Parsons, Bechtel, Toyota, Mitsubishi, Nissan, Charles Schwab and McKesson, as well as an estimated 2,000 smaller ones.

These departures have accompanied a distressing decline in the quality of employment for most Californians. Although overall California employment growth in the past decade has outperformed the rest of the country, most of the new jobs pay poorly. Overall, the state has created five times the number of low as opposed to high wage jobs. A remarkable 86 percent of all new jobs paid below the median income while almost half paid under $40,000. Even Silicon Valley has created fewer high-paying positions than the national average, and far fewer than prime competitors in places such as Salt Lake City, Seattle or Austin.[8]

Particularly hard-hit has been the industrial sector, the source of many well-paying blue-collar jobs. California lost 423,700 manufacturing jobs between 1991 and 2016.[9] Business-relocation expert Joe Vranich, who fled sunny Orange County for chilly Pittsburgh, Pennsylvania, notes such firms are particularly vulnerable to the state's regulatory-driven high energy prices. Since 2011, electricity prices have increased five times as fast as the national average.[10] Over the decade, California has fallen to the bottom half of states in terms of manufacturing employment growth, ranking a dismal 44th last year, with a new job creation one-third to one quarter that of growing states such as Texas, Virginia, Arizona, Nevada and Florida.[11]

The pandemic further accentuated the fragility of this bifurcated economy. The state's dependence on low-wage service workers, particularly in the hospitality industry, has been critical in the pandemic. However, California has among the highest unemployment rates in the nation, outdone only by tourism-dominated states like Hawaii and Nevada.[12] By early 2021, Los Angeles, the home of Hollywood, had the highest unemployment rate of the nation's top 10 metropolitan areas.[13]

As opportunities for upward mobility have dried up, state out-migration has mounted, with net domestic outmigration growing between 2014 and 2018 from 46,000 to 156,000. For the first time in a century, California actually has lost population. The conventional wisdom in Sacramento is that California mostly is losing its poor, elderly and less-skilled residents. Yet based on an analysis of IRS data from 2017-2018, only roughly one-third of those leaving the state made under $50,000 annually. Around two in five made over $100,000 and another quarter earned a middle-class paycheck between $50,000 and $100,000 annually. The fastest growth last decade among net leavers were those at the higher salary brackets.[14]

Perhaps the biggest concern is the loss of young people and families. The majority of people leaving the state come from those in the prime ages for raising families. Sadly, it is among both the young and the middle aged that out-migration is getting stronger.[15] This amounts to eating our own "seed corn." Los Angeles, notes the Brookings Institution's Bill Frey, suffered the biggest net loss of millennials of any region outside New York.[16]

California's dysfunctional demographics are the product not just of a lack of quality jobs, but of soaring housing prices, which are the nation's highest. In San Francisco, Los Angeles and San Diego, notes the Census, the 25-34 year-old home ownership rates range from 19.6 percent to 22.6 percent – approximately 40 percent or more below the national average.[17] California millennials on average earn about the same as their counterparts in less-expensive states such as Texas, Minnesota and Washington, where the cost of living is far lower.[18] The median home price in California statewide has topped an astounding $750,000 with median prices above $1 million in some coastal metro areas.[19]

The canary in the coalmine may be the drop in the number of foreign-born residents – the very group that made up for the state's long-term loss of domestic migrants. Over the past decade, Los Angeles has actually lost foreign-born population, which has stagnated in the San Francisco Bay Area, according to demographer Wendell Cox (author of Chapter Three). In contrast, red-state cities such as Dallas-Ft. Worth, Houston, Austin, Nashville and Columbus have experienced increases of between 20 percent and 40 percent of foreign-born residents.

California's major cities are becoming childless places. Los Angeles and San Francisco ranked among the bottom 10 in birthrates among the 53 major metropolitan areas in 2015 according to the American Community Survey.[20] The loss of young families and immigrants poses a unique challenge for California's economy, long dependent on innovation and historically the province of younger workers and entrepreneurs.[21] Cox calculates that since 2010, California's fertility rate has dropped 60 percent more than the national average and the state is now aging 50-percent more rapidly than the rest of the country. If these trends continue, wheelchairs will replace surfboards as state icons.[22]

A healthy state needs more job creation rather than better funding for pensions and more transfer payments. Yet new job creation is no priority, unless tied to government largesse. Other states would likely use a huge surplus to create new opportunities for middle-income jobs; California seems to have little interest in this.

Ecotopia: A Guidebook to the New Feudalism

California's path to what many see as a new feudalism may have been unintentional, but its roots lay, in large part, from its decision, starting in the early 1970s, to become the green role model for the planet. This shift started a half century ago, marked in part by the publishing of Stanford's Paul Ehrlich's 1968 jeremiad, *The Population Bomb*, which predicated environmental ruin and starvation in the near term.

These views gained acceptance in Sacramento with the elevation of Jerry Brown to the governorship in 1974. Brown spoke about "an era of limits" and sought to undermine the enormous growth machine built by his father. California's future direction was detailed in the science-fiction novel *Ecotopia*.[23]

The book follows a newspaper reporter who visits a breakaway republic whose policies in many ways presage the goals of today's environmental movement. *Ecotopia* reflects environmental concerns common in the 1970s – air pollution, energy dependence, pesticides, nuclear power and overpopulation.[24] Ecotopian policies resonate with extreme environmentalists today as they pursue a highly regulated, essentially socialistic society without cars, fossil fuels or air travel, and with limits placed on childbearing. Such thinking took deep roots among California's progressive leaders.

California's powerful green lobby has imposed a series of policies – on housing, transportation and energy – that are now being employed nationally such as the elimination of gas-powered cars by 2035 and a shift entirely to a fossil-fuels-free future. Such policies come at an enormous cost, as we've seen in California's economic travails.[25]

For California's leadership class, environmental catastrophism underpins all decision making. Not that this has made too much of a difference in terms of improving the climate. In the decade from 2007, after the Legislature passed the Golden State's "landmark" global-warming legislation, California has accounted for barely 5 percent of the nation's greenhouse-gas (GHG) reductions. The state ranks a mediocre 40th in per-capita GHG reduction over the past decade. State policies may actually be increasing the Earth's total emissions by pushing people and industries to states with more extreme climates.[26]

Towards the New Serfdom

The media and academia make little mention about how these green policies have proved catastrophic for the state's working and middle classes, driven the cost of energy and housing to unsustainable levels, and chased millions out of the state. In *Ecotopia*, at least, the burdens of the green regime were socially shared; while in the real California more Californians have fallen into energy poverty."[27]

California's green policies have been anything but socially democratic, instead being detrimental to many, if not most, California families. Pouring more money into transit – where $20 billion in spending has resulted in a smaller share of commuters than 30 years ago – is far less important than more prosaic things like fixing roads, filling potholes, and enhancing telecommuting. Rather than better roads, Californians get put on "road diets" that reduce road lanes and doom them to longer commutes.[28] Many of the state's "infrastructure" investments aren't about traditional infrastructure at all – but about funding transit, building bike lanes, restoring habitats and beautifying the highways.

Among the primary impacts of climate regulations has been to chase away historically well-paying jobs in fields such as manufacturing, energy and home building – all key employers for working- and middle-class Californians.[29] According to a recent United Way study, close to one in three families in the state is barely able to pay its bills.[30] Fully one-in-three welfare recipients in the nation lives in California, which is home to barely 12 percent of the country's population.[31]

Combined with households barely above the poverty line, 45.8 percent of California's children lived in or near poverty.[32] Subsidies and transfers are all that keeps many Californians from falling deeper into poverty.

Extreme poverty primarily is found in two places – California's vast interior regions and areas close to the urban cores. Anyone riding along Highway 33 through the San Joaquin Valley can see scenes that seem more like rural Mexico than America, with abandoned cars, dilapidated houses and deserted storefronts. Among the nation's 381 metropolitan areas, notes a recent Pew study, four of the 10 areas with the lowest share of middle class are in California's heartland – Fresno, Bakersfield, Visalia-Porterville and El Centro.[33] Three of the 10 regions with the highest proportion of poor people are also in the state's interior.[34] The Inland Empire east of Los Angeles has a population nearly as large as metropolitan Boston. It suffers the lowest average pay of any of the nation's 50 largest counties and among the highest poverty rates of any of the nation's 25 largest metropolitan areas.[35]

Urban California is home to similar scenes, even while remaining a favored locale for the ultra-rich. (Few of the very rich seem likely to choose Bakersfield or Fresno as their main residence). A new report by data firm Wealth-X suggests that there were 16,295 homeowners with a net worth of over $30 million in Los Angeles as of December 2020, which is the second-largest concentration in the world. Nevertheless, the city suffers the highest poverty rates for major U.S. metros. One in four Angelinos, according to a recent UCLA study, spend half their income on rent – the highest again of any major metropolitan area in the country.[36]

The hypocrisy on race is particularly revealing. No state advertises its multicultural bona fides more proudly than California. Latinos and African Americans constitute 45 percent of the total population.[37] Many of the state's lawmakers, for example, have endorsed reparations (although California was never a slave state) and is working to impose a "woke" agenda addressing "systemic" racism in its classrooms.[38] The state's leaders talk endlessly about helping its minority residents.

Rhetoric is one thing, but grassroots reality is another. Based on cost-of-living estimation tools from the Census Bureau, 28 percent of African Americans in the state live in poverty, compared with 22 percent nationally.[39] One-third of Latinos, now the state's largest ethnic group, live in poverty, compared with 21 percent outside the state.[40] Of the 331 zip codes making up the top 1 percent of overcrowded zip codes in the United States, 134 are in Southern California, primarily in greater Los Angeles and San Diego – mostly concentrated around heavily Latino areas such as Pico-Union, East Los Angeles and Santa Ana in Orange County.[41]

In the past, poor Californians, whether from the Deep South, Mexico or the Dust Bowl, could count on the state's once exemplary education system to help them move up. Now California has among the lowest reading scores for eighth graders in the nation. Latino academic achievement is generally lower than in the rest of the nation.[42] Much data suggests that the state's tough public-school lockdowns have harmed minority and poor students the most – and teachers' unions have consistently dragged their feet on a return to in-classroom learning. Minorities are also the prime victims of the now rising violent crime. Majority-minority Los Angeles County is by some measurements home to the top three most unsafe neighborhoods in the country.[43]

Rather than harbinger of a more democratic capitalism, California now has become what author Antonio Garcia Martinez has labelled "feudalism with better marketing."[44] At the top of the hierarchy, the tech companies' capital gains and IPOs have been able to fund California's welfare state, which continues to grow as the economy bifurcates. The state budget is awash in cash thanks to our steeply progressive income-tax system. This largesse allows the state to continue doling out money – by 2021 the state was issuing checks or aiding two out of every three Californians, while bailing out much of the state's impoverished renters by allowing them not to pay full rent, a disaster particularly for small, not highly capitalized owners.[45]

Rather than fight inequality, the tech billionaires are seeking ways to accommodate it. Gregory Ferenstein, who interviewed 147 digital company founders, says most believe that, "An increasingly greater share of economic wealth will be generated by a smaller slice of very talented or original people. Everyone else will increasingly subsist on some combination of part-time entrepreneurial 'gig work' and government aid."[46] Many of them, and their progressive backers, would like such regular transfers to become permanent and favor a publicly-funded guaranteed annual wage to help, in part, allay insurrectional fears about the "disruption" on a potentially exposed workforce.[47] We're seeing such a development nationwide, but nowhere is it more obvious than in tech-oriented California.

Is There a Way Back?

Innovation remains deeply rooted in the state's DNA. The state still has some lovely neighborhoods, the nation's dominant port, Hollywood's film industry and countless legacy industries, including in global-leading space exploration.[48] The weather remains unsurpassed, the beaches alluring and the topography still is spectacular. Californians can only broadly enjoy this bounty when they realize that a pronounced public-policy change is necessary.

Most young people in the state already believe that they will never be better off than their parents.[49] The resulting resentments may not be articulated, but they definitely lie under the surface. More Californians believe that the state is heading in the wrong direction than in the right one, according to a recent Public Policy Institute of California poll – a number that reaches above 55 percent in the poorer inland areas.[50] Critically, there are signs of pushback in minority business communities over such things as the state's natural gas ban.[51] In 2020, for instance, 200 veteran civil rights leaders sued the California Air Resources Board, on the basis that the state air-quality policies skew against poor and minority residents.[52]

Reversing policies in a state with a large and powerful contingent of people who are dependent on public largesse, including the politically powerful and reform-resistant public-sector unions, won't be easy. But the time is now for California to put aside its ecotopian dogmas and find ways to slow our drift towards an increasingly divided state.

Ultimately, California needs to confront its biggest problem: the lack of high-paying private sector jobs. The current approach focuses on subsidy, which may be understandable in a public-health emergency but is becoming the permanent feature of the state's economy. The unsustainable nature of this reality will become clearer when the current IPO and capital gains tsunami wears off, as is inevitable.

Some steps toward improvement

Here are a few small steps the state can take to reverse course. They are aimed at reducing costs and at boosting the productive capacity of our citizens. The main step is much larger, of course, and involves convincing California's leaders to recognize the degree to which their environmental fixations and tax and regulatory policies drive up the cost of living and reduce business opportunities – and end up hurting poor and minority residents the most.

First, the state should use the current $75.7-billion surplus to develop worker-training programs tied to new investments in downtrodden areas. Some conservative states such as Ohio, Texas, Tennessee and South Carolina have lured private investments by providing not just reduced taxes and infrastructure, but state-supported skills training. States like Ohio prioritize training for blue-collar skills, one of the prime reasons companies locate there.

California high schools, in contrast, have focused on encouraging all students to attend four-year colleges such as University of California and California State University schools, which makes little sense for many and does not lead to the same results. In Virginia, Colorado and Texas, where the state tracks earnings, students with certain technically oriented credentials short of bachelor's degrees earn an average of $2,000 to $11,000 a year more than bachelor's degree-holders, the American Institutes for Research found.[53]

Second, the state should consider a wide-ranging tax-rebate program to lure large-scale investments into poor areas such as south Los Angeles and the Central Valley. Such investments have helped turn local economies around, as seen in San Antonio, Texas. It's better to provide incentives – and even provide targeted subsidies, when appropriate – that lure upwardly mobile jobs to hard-pressed communities than keep people on the dole permanently. In San Antonio, as former Mayor Henry Cisneros suggests, the location of a new Toyota plant helped create prosperity for what had been a poor, military dominated city.[54]

Third, California should stop the climate virtue signaling and instead embrace growth-oriented environmental policies. In adopting draconian regulations not adopted by other states and countries, notably China, California is chasing people and companies to countries with higher rates of emissions. Instead, the state should look at incremental ways to reduce greenhouse gases that do not cause so much collateral damage to middle- and working-class Californians.

This includes such policies as encouraging the dispersion of work to homes or places close to where most California families can afford to live. In particular, the state needs to remove its current emphasis on reducing Vehicle Miles Traveled, which makes developing in the interior much easier. The notion that Californians will shift to mass transit has proven cruelly off base; the current policy discriminates against the middle and working class while doing little to reduce emissions, outside of persuading people and companies to leave the state.[55]

Fourth, the Legislature needs to prioritize reform of the California Environmental Quality Act (CEQA). State policymakers from both parties have often complained about the ill effects of the "landmark" 1970 law, which makes it too easy for anti-growth groups or unions seeking to hobble competitors to file lawsuits that delay or even stop needed housing projects. Some 60 percent of all lawsuits involve housing projects, according to a recent study. After new housing is finally approved, any party can – even anonymously – file a CEQA lawsuit seeking to block the housing for "environmental" reasons, resulting in costly, multi-year delays, one reason why California produces far less housing per capita than rival states like Texas.[56]

Finally, California needs to reform its tax system so that there is an incentive to create jobs and housing. The current system is too reliant on sales taxes at a time when much of brick-and-mortar retail is collapsing. Cities should receive incentives to turn redundant retail into housing and other productive uses. The current tax system discourages this. More important, the state needs to rebuild its most critical resource – middle-class families who can support themselves and diversify the tax base. Right now, the top 1 percent pay close to half of all state taxes. California has put itself in the position where the only way it can boost revenues would be to tax more of those who fund it, with the possible impact of forcing them to leave for elsewhere.[57]

Joel Kotkin is a fellow in urban studies at Chapman University in Orange. He writes about demographic, social, and economic trends in the U.S. and internationally.

CHAPTER TWO: CALIFORNIA'S HOUSING CRISIS

CHAPTER TWO
CALIFORNIA'S HOUSING CRISIS

By Wendell Cox

*The affordability of housing is overwhelmingly
a function of just one thing, the extent to which
governments place artificial restrictions on the supply of
residential land.*

> —*Donald Brash, Governor,*
> *Reserve Bank of New Zealand*
> *(1988-2002)*

There is probably no issue more requiring resolution in California than poor housing affordability. It is a threat to the preservation of the middle-class and the competitiveness of the state.

Housing affordability is more than house prices – it is house prices *in relation to income*. Price-to-income ratios are widely used, such as by the World Bank, the Organization for International Cooperation and Development and others to measure housing affordability. This chapter uses the "median multiple," a price-to-income ratio (median house price divided by the gross median household income) to measure middle-income housing affordability (Table 1).

TABLE 1
Demographia Housing Affordability Ratings

Housing Affordability Rating	Median Multiple
Affordable	3.0 & Under
Moderately Unaffordable	3.1 to 4.0
Seriously Unaffordable	4.1 to 5.0
Severely Unaffordable	5.1 & Over

Median multiple: Median house price divided by median household income

Housing affordability herein is at the housing market level – the metropolitan area, which is both a housing market and labor (commuting) market.[1] This excludes submarkets, such as municipalities or neighborhoods.

Housing affordability is compared (1) *between* housing markets (such as between the San Francisco metropolitan area and the Dallas-Fort Worth metropolitan area) or (2) over years *within* the same housing market (such as in the San Francisco metropolitan area).

California Housing Affordability in Context

Until about 1970, housing was affordable (less than 3.0 median multiple) throughout the United States, including California. All but one of today's 53 major markets[2] was rated "Affordable." Since then, huge housing affordability differences have arisen, especially between California and the nation (Figure 1). This has been due to much higher land costs, as construction costs have risen more modestly.[3]

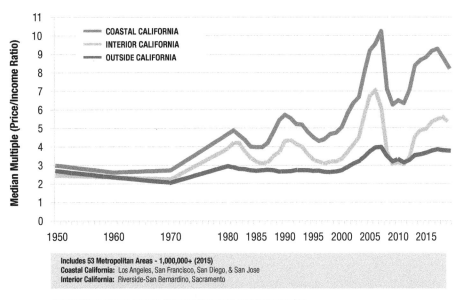

FIGURE 1
California and the United States Compared
Middle Income Housing Affordability: 1950–2019

Includes 53 Metropolitan Areas - 1,000,000+ (2015)
Coastal California: Los Angeles, San Francisco, San Diego, & San Jose
Interior California: Riverside-San Bernardino, Sacramento

Derived from Census Bureau, Harvard University and Demographia.

The Legislative Analyst's Office reports that an average California home costs 2.5 times the national average and monthly rent is about 50 percent higher.[4] In 2019, the median California house value was $325,000 above the US median.

In 2019, California's major coastal markets were the least affordable in the nation.[5] Los Angeles had a median multiple of 9.0, San Francisco 8.5, San Jose 8.4 and San Diego 8.0. This compares to Seattle, the least affordable outside California, though still severely unaffordable (5.5).[6] Housing was severely unaffordable even in the interior markets, with Riverside-San Bernardino at 5.4 and Sacramento at 5.2.[7]

Mortgage Qualification and Incomes: In the four coastal markets, most middle-income households have insufficient incomes to qualify for a mortgage on a median priced house with a 10 percent down payment.[8] Qualification would be limited to the top 18.6 percent of the middle-income distribution in San Diego, 16.8 percent in Los Angeles and 5.0 percent in San Francisco. No middle-income households in San Jose would be eligible.

The median income San Jose household would need $149,000 more income to qualify for the median priced house, in San Francisco $107,000, Los Angeles $58,000 and San Diego $54,000 (Table 2).

Outside California, the situation is much brighter, with 72 percent of the middle-income distribution qualifying. The median income household qualifies for a mortgage on the median priced house in 38 of 45 major markets, compared to none of the six in California.

TABLE 2
Mortgage Qualification Data: Median Priced House: 2019
51 Major Housing Markets for Which Data is Available

Markets	% of Middle-Income Distribution with Qualifying Income	Additional Income Required for Median Income Household to Qualify
MAJOR MARKETS INTERIOR CALIFORNIA	54.8%	$6,750
Sacramento	58.2%	$4,400
Riverside-San Bernardino	51.4%	$9,100
MAJOR MARKETS COASTAL CALIFORNIA	13.5%	$91,950
San Diego	18.6%	$54,000
Los Angeles	16.8%	$57,800
San Francisco	5.0%	$106,600
San Jose	0.0%	$149,400
MAJOR MARKETS OUTSIDE CALIFORNIA	72.0%	$11,362
Rated Severely Unaffordable	52.2%	-$12,800
Rated Seriously Unaffordable	66.9%	$5,700
Rated Moderately Unaffordable	76.2%	$14,600
Rated Affordable	86.1%	$22,700

Derived from National Association of Realtors, American Community Survey and Demographia data.

Assumes 10% down payment and contemporary mortgage interest rate.

The 2020 *Economic Report of the President*[9] found "a house price premium resulting from excessive housing regulation" of from 100 percent in the Los Angeles and San Diego metros and 150 percent in the San Francisco Bay Area. This report notes the high prices drove rents up as well.[10]

California's severely unaffordable housing materially reduces the value of its high incomes. Despite its high household income, metro San Jose's standard of living index ranks 46th out of the 107 metropolitan areas over 500,000. Metro San Francisco is 58th. San Diego's ranks 90th, and Los Angeles is nearly at the bottom, at 104th. More than 85 percent of the cost-of-living difference between the more expensive metros and the national average is in housing costs.[11] California's excessively high cost of living is a formidable barrier for middle-income and hopeless for lower-income households.

Land Use Regulation in California

Economic research attributes California's housing affordability crisis to stronger land-use regulation starting around 1970.[12]

Dartmouth economist William Fischel published an early seminal review[13] of housing affordability in California (1970 to the 1990s). Fischel suggested that regulatory research should look for major changes that "are adopted in some places but not in others."

Fischel examined the higher house price increases that occurred in California compared to the rest of the nation between the late 1960s and late 1980s. Fischel cites various possible causal factors. He found that the higher prices could not be explained by higher construction cost increases, demand, higher personal income growth, the quality of life, amenities, Proposition 13, land supply or water issues.

Instead Fischel cites stronger land use restrictions. There were two principal issues, the California Environmental Quality Act (CEQA) and local growth management restrictions.[14]

Growth Control: Fischel notes that California "became the leader in the 'growth control,'"[15] a new land-use strategy that limited new housing development (especially "greenfield" development). According to Fischel, under growth management, "Allowable growth is held below the rate that was both permitted under previous zoning laws and below the rate at the community's vacant land inventory can reasonably sustain." Growth management could impose building moratoria, annual quotas and limits on conversion of vacant land to housing.[16]

Fischel contrasts growth management with "ordinary zoning, which is nominally dedicated to the good-housekeeping rule of a 'place for everything, but everything in its place.'" In contrast, "growth-control communities attempt to reduce future residential development." "Growth management" regulations were superimposed by municipalities upon their ordinary zoning. Before the later evolution of growth management to counties and housing markets, builders could "shop around" for more affordable municipal regulatory environments.

The California Environmental Quality Act: CEQA imposed far stronger environmental reviews for private housing projects than elsewhere. Under CEQA, anti-development interests routinely challenged major "greenfield"[17] housing projects. Some projects have been blocked, others have been delayed for decades[18] and become far more costly through the CEQA process. As regards its effect on greenfield development, CEQA has effectively acted as urban containment.

Other early research raised concerns. Massachusetts Institute of Technology professor Bernard J. Frieden noted in 1979, "the public benefits are small, costs to the consumer's big and inequities unmistakable."[19] David E. Dowell, a University of California economist found that "wherever stringent land-use controls have come up against burgeoning demand for housing, land and home prices have skyrocketed."[20]

Impact Fees: In response to Proposition 13, the 1978 ballot measure that largely limited property taxes to 1 percent of the purchase price, municipalities began to use impact fees on new houses and apartments to fund new development. Single-family fees average four times ($28,000) the rest of the nation.[21] Fees range to more than $150,000 per house.

There are huge impact fee variations between municipalities[22] and questions about the "nexus" between such fees and new development.[23] At the same time that costs for new development have been transferred to new owners,[24] existing owners received, in effect, windfall profits from extraordinary house value increases in California's regulatory environment.

From Municipal Regulation to Housing Market Regulation: Growth management started as a municipal issue. However, it expanded to cover counties and entire housing markets.[25]

The balance between supply and demand has been upset by seriously restricting land for residential development, at the same time as demand increased. This, as predicted by economics, leads to higher prices, all else being equal.

Dynamics of Urban Land Markets

Harvard's William Alonso showed that the value of residential land tends to increase from the rural uses on the urban fringe[26] to centers of economic activity, such as central business districts.[27]

Urban Containment: Urban containment has become the dominant planning strategy for combating urban expansion and has been implemented in California through CEQA[28] and growth management restrictions.

According to prominent urban planners Arthur C. Nelson and Casey J. Dawkins: "urban containment involves drawing a line around an urban area. Urban development is steered to the area inside the line and discouraged (if not prevented) outside it."[29] Further: "urban containment programs can be distinguished from traditional approaches to land use regulation by the presence of policies that are explicitly designed to limit the development of land outside a defined urban area, while encouraging infill development and redevelopment inside the urban area."[30]

Urban containment is intended to increase land costs. According to Nelson and Dawkins, "the regional demand for urban development is shifted to the area inside the boundary. This shift should decrease the value of land outside the boundary and increase the value of land inside the boundary."[31]

The impact of urban containment on urban land is illustrated in Figure 2. The land value increases inside the urban growth boundary (UGB) are the "urban containment effect."[32] Other land value increases from land use regulation, such as "ordinary zoning" would be *in addition to* higher values from the urban containment effect.

Thus, the operative dynamics of urban containment are that:

1. Land values rise precipitously at urban growth boundaries (or their equivalent).

2. This increase is telescoped onto virtually all plots inside UGBs, raising house prices.

FIGURE 2
Urban Containment Effect on Land Value
EXAMPLE OF URBAN GROWTH BOUNDARY

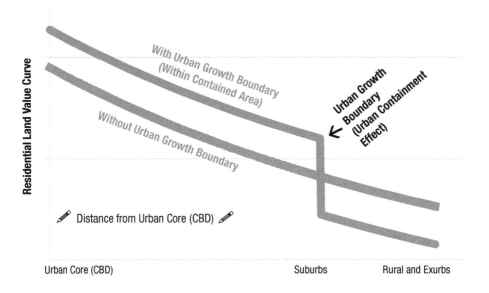

There was, however, a risk. Nelson and Dawkins note that "higher prices (especially for housing) could occur if planning fails to increase the supply of buildable land within the boundary" and that "urban containment boundaries are prudent land-use policies ... only when accompanied by policies that increase urban development density and intensity."[33] Housing affordability would be preserved by expanding urban containment boundaries "to accommodate projected growth over a specified future time period, typically 10 to 20 years."[34]

URBAN SPRAWL IN CALIFORNIA

Urban planning has been pre-occupied with curbing urban expansion, popularly called "urban sprawl," and has embraced urban containment as a principal solution. Regrettably, urban containment is strongly associated with severely unaffordable housing and its consequences (below).

Paradoxically, California is the *least sprawling* of any state. California has the highest urban densities, at 4,304 residents per square mile in 2010. New York ranks second, at 4,161. Further, California's density of new urban development was more than double that of any other state and more than 5.5 times the national average between 2000 and 2010.[35] The three densest large urban areas in the United States are Los Angeles, San Francisco and San Jose, all denser, perhaps surprisingly, than New York.

Elusive Densification: However, sufficient densification did not occur. Perhaps the "social engineering" required to force households into smaller, often multi-family housing was politically infeasible.

Without the massive densification that would have been required to preserve housing affordability, it is not surprising that considerable political pressure has been directed toward reform of single-family zoning (an ordinary zoning measure) in markets with urban containment. As house prices have risen, so have rents (though at a slower rate[36]).

However, replacement of single-family zoning may not lead to materially improved housing affordability.

For example, the city of Vancouver, British Columbia has virtually eliminated single-family zoning[37] and massively densified, increasing its population 65 percent from 1961 to 2016,[38] without material annexation or greenfield capacity.

University of British Columbia planning Professor Patrick Condon, who has studied Vancouver extensively, has concluded "there is a problem beyond restrictive zoning. … No amount of opening zoning or allowing for development will cause prices to go down."[39] The problem, according to Condon, is that upzoning as a densification strategy does not improve housing affordability.[40]

Despite the densification, the Vancouver housing market had experienced massive housing affordability losses. Metro Vancouver has the highest house prices and highest rents in Canada.[41] Further, Vancouver is the second least affordable market in the *Demographia International Housing Affordability*. Affordability has worsened from a 3.9 median multiple in 1970[42] to 13.0 in 2020. Metro Vancouver has had stringent urban containment policies for decades.

The housing affordability (median multiple) range was far less when there was only ordinary zoning. Median multiples in major U.S. markets did not rise above 4.0 until urban containment.[43] In 2019, the 12 least affordable markets had median multiples from 5.1 to 9.0, and all had urban containment.[44]

Moreover, examination of US data suggests *this opposite relationship*. Metros with *more* single-family housing and *larger* lot sizes (both indicators of *lower* density) have substantially better housing affordability (Table 3).

- San Diego, San Jose, San Francisco and Los Angeles ranked 44th through 47th in their shares of single-family housing.[45]

- Some of the smallest lot sizes were in San Diego (42nd), Los Angeles (47th), San Jose (48th) and San Francisco (50th).[46]

TABLE 3
Single Family Houses & Lot Sizes
Major Metropolitan Areas: By Affordability Ratings (2018)

Housing Markets (Metro Areas): Number by Affordability Rating (Median Multiples shown)	Single Family Share of All Housing Units	Single Family Housing Average Lot Size (Acres)
Affordable (3.0 & Lower)	66.1%	0.34
Moderately Unaffordable (3.1 - 4.0)	61.7%	0.30
Seriously Unaffordable (4.1 - 5.0)	60.4%	0.24
Severely Unaffordable (5.0 & Higher)	53.7%	0.19
Number of Housing Markets with Data	53	50

Sources:
Affordability Data: American Community Survey 2018 (Census Bureau), Demographia International Housing Affordability. Lot Sizes: American Housing Survey: 2011 & 2013 (Census Bureau)

Contravening Land Market Dynamics: Often urban containment requires new development to be adjacent to existing development. One of
the world's leading urban and housing analysts, New York University Marr-
ron Institute Director of Urban Expansion, Shlomo Angel explains the problem with this approach.

"If only plots that were directly adjacent to existing built-up areas were
allowed to develop, their owners would have monopolistic power. For the
land market on the urban periphery to function properly, supply must be
adequate to allow competition to determine land prices."[47]

This could lead to the virtual destruction of the competitive supply of
land, which Brookings Institution economist Anthony Downs stressed is
required to maintain housing affordability. Legendary British planner Peter
Hall[48] and colleagues at University College London expressed concern that
land-use plans could "act as a speculator's guide." Land with planning permission or likely planning permission becomes a desirable item which will
be traded at increasing prices or hoarded."[49]

Urban Containment Research: In fact, urban containment has been associated with deteriorated housing affordability.

- According to Angel, "the explicit containment of urban expansion by greenbelts, as in Seoul, Korea or in English cities, by
  urban growth boundaries, as in Portland, Oregon, or by environmental restrictions as in California – has inevitably been
  associated with declines in housing affordability."

- Hall, et al suggested that by the early 1970s, the "speculative value" of land with planning permission in the UK was five to 10
  times that of land without planning permission.[50] They also concluded that the failure to prevent housing affordability losses
  was "perhaps the biggest single failure" of urban containment
  in the UK.

- Mariano Kulish, Anthony Richards and Christian Gillitzer of the
  Reserve Bank of Australia report that that land increased in val-
  ue from 12 to 20 times when brought within the Melbourne
  UGB.[51]

- Arthur Grimes, former chair of the Board of the Reserve Bank of New Zealand, and Yun Liang found a land value gap of 7.9 to 13.1 times over the Auckland UGB.[52]

- Gerald Mildner of Portland State University found that a gap in land values of 10 times across the UGB in Portland.[53]

- The Barker Reviews indicated that land on which housing was permitted had a value of more than 250 times that of the agricultural land outside London where housing was not permitted.[54]

- Benjamin Dachis of the C. D. Howe Institute has associated administration of Toronto's urban containment (greenbelt) program with far higher house prices.[55] By 2020, the median multiple had reached 250 percent of its 2004 (pre-urban containment) level.[56]

Prominent housing economists Edward Glaeser of Harvard and Joseph Gyourko of the University of Pennsylvania presented evidence in the San Francisco metropolitan area (city of San Francisco and suburbs) that land values[57] were approximately $490,000, or 10 times ($440,000) the expected 20 percent in a well-functioning market. Much of this additional cost is attributable to urban containment.

Where there is severely unaffordable housing, urban containment tends to be present.[58] This includes some major markets in the United States and Canada, as well as virtually all major markets in Australia, the United Kingdom and New Zealand. All 92 severely unaffordable major markets in the *Demographia International Housing Affordability* have urban containment.

Angel, an advocate of densification, has strong reservations about urban containment, says that, "You have to show me that you have enough room that you are creating for the demand for me to say it's okay to have containment, but usually you can't. So, what it means is that you need expansion."[59]

Urban containment may be the "critical mass" that explains much of the housing affordability crisis in the least affordable markets, including California. (Other explanations are evaluated in Box 2.)

Indeed, economist Claude Gruen observed, "growth controls in economically powerful coastal cities is to the middle-class what the economic disaster of slum clearance was to the poor."[60]

There are other views on the causes of California's housing affordability crisis.

Shortage of Developable Land: In the San Francisco Bay Area, for example, the high house prices are often blamed on a shortage of land. However, there is no shortage of agricultural land, which has typically been used for new urban development. In 2017, the total agricultural land in just the San Francisco and San Jose metropolitan areas alone was equal to 150 percent of the urbanized land.[61]

As a matter of interest, geographer John Fraser Hart of the University of Minnesota has noted that, "The loss of cropland to suburban encroachment may be cause for intense local concern, but attempts to thwart development cannot be justified on grounds of a net national loss of good cropland.[62]

Moreover, agricultural land costs have increased 30 percent per acre since 1969,[63] far less than the nine times increase in land values.[64] The 2017 value of agricultural land averaged $1,800 per quarter acre,[65] far less than the average quarter acre residential lot in the San Francisco ($900,000) and San Jose metropolitan areas ($1,200,000) – from 500 to more than 660 times agricultural values.[66] The "land shortage" results from public policy, not topography.

Demand: Housing affordability deterioration is frequently blamed on increased demand, especially by international interests, major investors and investment or "speculation." Demand generally leads to higher prices only if there is not enough supply, which makes it more difficult to build houses affordable to middle-income households. Housing affordability can then worsen further, as demand continues to increase, without sufficient supply enhancement.

Truths and Consequences

Urban containment has significant costs. In commenting on the association between London's urban growth boundary,[67] and the higher costs of housing, *The Economist* said: "Suburbs rarely cease growing of their own accord. The only reliable way to stop them, it turns out, is to stop them forcefully. But the consequences of doing that are severe."[68] These are evident in California:

- *Middle-Income Housing Affordability:* Downs noted that even a 10 percent increase in house prices is "socially significant" because of the number of households it denies home ownership.[69] As the *Economic Report of the President* shows, this is a price premium long since exceeded in California.[70]

- *High poverty rates:* California is testimony to those consequences, with the highest cost-of–living-adjusted poverty rate of any state (including better-known centers of poverty, like Mississippi and West Virginia).[71]

- *Worsening Inequality:* By definition, as housing affordability becomes more severe, inequality is increased, because fewer households can afford the higher prices. Some are forced to seek housing subsidies, which can require years on waiting lists, assuming that waiting lists are open. For example, *all* nine waiting lists are closed in the city of San Francisco.[72] And, as noted above, nearly all of the cost-of-living difference between high-cost metros and the national average is explained by higher housing costs.[73] Moreover, higher cost housing has resulted in a massive intergenerational wealth transfer, as existing owners have reaped huge gains in house values, which has severely limited homeownership among younger households. Unaffordable housing is a *principal driver of rising inequality.*

- *Retarded Economic Growth:* Research indicates that tighter land-use regulation has diminished national economic growth, while relaxation could produce "significant growth effects."[74] One estimate indicates that US labor productivity would be 12.4 percent higher if states rolled back their housing regulation levels to the Texas level.[75]

- *Declining population growth and increasing domestic migration:* For nearly all of the 20th century, California was the national growth leader. In every census from 1930 to 2000, California added more residents than any other state. In 1900, California ranked 21st in population. By 1970, it had reached the top position, which it has occupied since that time. But much has changed since then. California lost 70,000 residents in 2019-20, and there has been a net outflow of residents to other states of 2.7 million since 2000,[76] as housing affordability has deteriorated.

Without restoring the competitive supply of land on the urban fringe, material improvement in housing affordability is likely impossible. Indeed, the prospect is for further worsening, with pent-up demand driving prices even higher.

A Way Forward: The Housing Opportunity Area

Solving California's housing crisis will require addressing the root of the problem–land values have risen to a point that prevents production for all but the most affluent middle-income households in the four coastal markets.

However, though housing is severely unaffordable in the interior markets, it is far better than on the coast. There may be an opportunity to stop further affordability retardation, by preserving a modicum of middle-income affordability, while giving businesses a relocation area sufficiently competitive relative with other states.

A Housing Opportunity Area

The Legislature should create a "Housing Opportunity Area" (HOA) in the interior to restore the competitive market for land, thereby preventing further deterioration in housing affordability.

Geographical Extent: The HOA would include the San Joaquin and Sacramento valley counties from Shasta to Kern, as well as San Bernardino, Riverside and Imperial and Antelope Valley in Los Angeles County.[77]

Regulation in the HOA: Land-use regulation in the HOA would be liberalized.[78] The HOA would be exempt from urban containment, and other post-1970 regulations associated with undermining the competitive market for land. Like the CEQA streamlining authorized for subsidized low-income housing in Senate Bill 7 (2021),[79] HOA supporters propose that zoning and land-use regulatory streamlining would apply to middle-income and low-income greenfield projects. Authorization would be virtually automatic for developments of, say, at least 50-plus houses or apartments, that is to be served by infrastructure (public or private). Adjacent development *would not* be required, though reasonable detached housing maximum lot sizes would be allowed (consistent with California's historic small lot sizes). This type of development would be particularly appropriate given the current shift to much greater remote working.

Effect: Prevention of further housing affordability deterioration would provide an otherwise fleeting opportunity for middle-income households to achieve the California Dream of homeownership, rather than leave California. Moreover, the stronger economic and housing affordability in the interior could unleash competitive pressures on the coastal markets that could influence better housing affordability.

The HOA would be transformational but is the type of root-cause solution that may be necessary to address California's housing crisis.

Impact Fee Reform: Costs of new development have been shifted from all property owners to owners of newly developed property (such as houses), through the use of municipal impact fees. Meanwhile, existing house values have skyrocketed in California. Some of the gains by existing homeowners are, in effect, transferred from new home buyers paying higher house prices. This worsens housing affordability. The state should transfer these "costs of growth" from new owners to the general tax base.

A Final Thought

The major regulatory changes adopted in California but not in most other places have been widespread urban containment (growth control and CEQA) at the housing market level and, to a lesser extent, the excessively high municipal impact fees. The association between these strategies and deteriorated housing affordability is clear.

Wendell Cox is principal of Demographia, an international public policy firm located in the St. Louis metropolitan area. He is a founding senior fellow at the Urban Reform Institute, Houston, a senior fellow with the Frontier Centre for Public Policy in Winnipeg and a member of the Advisory Board of the Center for Demographics and Policy at Chapman University in Orange, California. He has been author or co-author of the 17 annual "Demographia International Housina Affordability" reports.

CHAPTER THREE: CALIFORNIA ON THE STREETS

CHAPTER THREE
CALIFORNIA ON THE STREETS

By Wayne Winegarden

It's a disgrace that the richest state, in the richest nation –
succeeding across so many sectors – is falling so far behind
to properly house, heal and humanely treat so many of its
own people. Every day, the California dream is dimmed by
the wrenching reality of families, children, and senior[s]
living unfed on a concrete bed.
— *Gov. Gavin Newsom*

Governor Newsom is correct. California's homeless crisis is a disgrace.

Whether in Los Angeles, San Francisco or any other major metropolitan area, the consequences from California's homelessness crisis are overwhelming. Given the current direness of the situation, it is easy to forget that the number of homeless people was actually declining not so long ago.

With the onset of the subprime mortgage crisis in 2007, California's homeless population was 139,000.[1] The number steadily declined afterward, just like the rest of the country, and reached a low of approximately 114,000 people by 2014. Unlike the rest of the country, this was as good as it would get.

Although the problem continued to improve almost everywhere else, California's crisis has only worsened. By 2020, the latest federal Housing and Urban Development data available as of this writing, the number of homeless has reached 161,548 people.

California has spent billions of dollars trying to address the problem, yet the state is no closer to winning this war. Despite these failures, many politicians continue to believe that taxpayers should throw even more money at the problem as if homelessness festers due to a lack of funding – not the state's errant approach.

According to the California State Auditor's office, over the past three years at least nine state agencies have spent $13 billion via 41 programs to alleviate the homelessness problem.[2] Relative to the average number of people living on the streets between 2018 and 2020, this is the equivalent of spending more than $30,000 per homeless person over these three years. These expenditures do not include the money local governments have spent or the spending of other agencies (like hospitals and law enforcement) when they are interacting with the homeless.

The auditor's report also admonishes California's "struggle to coordinate its efforts to address homelessness," claiming its "approach … is disjointed". As for the Homeless Coordinating and Financing Council set up in 2017, the auditor notes that it "cannot coordinate existing state and federal funding because it lacks expenditure data from state agencies."

California's state bureaucracy is demonstrating an inability to stem the growth in homelessness let alone alleviate the crisis. Rather than California's current government-centric disjointed approach, sustainably addressing California's crisis requires reforms that:

- Repeal the policies that make California an unaffordable place to live;

- Focus resources on supporting private nonprofits that address the root causes of homelessness in addition to connecting them with appropriate housing;

- Better leverage state resources, such as local law enforcement, to help connect homeless people with the resources and private nonprofits that can help; and,

- Repeal or reform initiatives, like Proposition 47, in coordination with implementing homeless courts in order to help homeless people get the support they need more efficiently.

Understanding the Crisis

Before discussing policies that address the problem, it is necessary to document the causes of the crisis, which are multi-dimensional.

From an economic perspective, the problem is straightforward: California's policies make it an unaffordable place to live. There are many ways to document California's lack of affordability. From a broad perspective, the Federal Reserve Bank of St. Louis (FRB-SL) maintains a database that compares the cost of living for each state.[3] Based on the data for 2018, California is the third most-expensive state behind Hawaii and New York.

While all costs are above average, California's largest drivers are excessive rent and housing expenses. As the California Budget & Policy Center put it,

> More than four in 10 households statewide had unaffordable housing costs in 2017. Furthermore, one in 5 households across California faced severe housing cost burdens, spending more than half of their income toward housing expenses.[4]

It is noteworthy that housing unaffordability was improving following the mortgage crisis but started becoming unaffordable around 2014 – the time that California's homeless problem started worsening.

California's unaffordable housing is a policy choice, although an unintentional one. Housing supply is severely constrained thanks to overly restrictive zoning regulations, exploitation of the California Environmental Quality Act (CEQA), overly burdensome review processes and ill-advised rent-control policies that depress the supply of rental housing. Throw in costly environmental regulations, including the new solar mandate on all newly built homes, and affordable housing has become an oxymoron.

Housing costs are not the only driver of California's unaffordability problem. According to the Council for Community and Economic Research,[5] three California regions qualified for the top 10 most expensive urban areas as of 2020. San Francisco is the third-most expensive (behind only the Manhattan borough of New York City and Honolulu), Oakland is the seventh-most expensive area, and Orange County is the eighth-most expensive.

The consequence of this elevated cost of living is that California's median income is not as high as it appears. According to the U.S. Census, the median household income in California was $70,038 in 2017 and $78,105 in 2019, the latest data available as of this writing.[6] Adjusted for buying power, California's median household income was estimated to be $58,967 in 2017 – 15.8 percent lower than the official estimate from the U.S. Census. This adjustment also drops California's ranking. Adjusting the state's 12th-highest income for how far that income goes, the purchasing power of California's median income is only the 24th-highest in the country.

With respect to the homeless crisis, California's unaffordability pushes significantly more people and families to the edge. Californians, particularly low-income Californians, are more likely to fall into a vicious cycle from unexpected financial burdens or adverse life events that people in other states would be able to successfully navigate. This increased vulnerability to financial shocks manifests itself into a larger number of people who are homeless for economic reasons. High housing costs, which often lead to bidding wars for homes, also make it more difficult for nonprofit groups that serve the homeless to find affordable properties.

Homelessness is not just an economic issue; many would argue it is not even primarily an economic issue. Whether it is a small minority or a large majority, the large number of people living on the streets who are suffering from mental illness or problems with substance abuse is well documented.[7] Mental illness and substance abuse are not new, but how California addresses these problems has changed. These changes were implemented right around the time of the rise in the state's homeless population – just like with the problem of housing affordability.

Recent legal rulings and policy changes are establishing a de facto right to sleep on the street and discouraging the enforcement of petty property crimes. The combination of these changes better enables people who are struggling with mental illness and substance abuse problems to remain on the streets rather than seek help.

Regarding the right to sleep on the street, the recent federal appeals court ruling *Martin v. City of Boise* is seminal. As John Hirschauer explains in *National Review*, "(I)n making its decision, the Ninth Circuit weighed, in the majority's words, 'whether the Eighth Amendment's prohibition on cruel and unusual punishment bars a city from prosecuting people criminally for sleeping outside on public property when those people have no home or other shelter to go to.'"[8] As it has been applied, this ruling is essentially prohibiting cities from enforcing laws against sleeping outside on public property unless adequate shelter beds exist. Since confirming this fact is difficult, the ruling has created an effective right to live on the sidewalks.

Then there is the seemingly unrelated Proposition 47. Among its provisions, Prop. 47, passed in November 2014, lowered the penalties for drug and property crimes. With respect to property crimes, Prop. 47 raised the theft threshold to $950 and thereby made larceny below this threshold a misdemeanor not a felony. Unsurprisingly, lowering the punishment for larceny has encouraged more theft and discouraged enforcement of the law.[9]

The Public Policy Institute of California found evidence that "property crime increased after 2014. While the reform had no apparent impact on burglaries or auto thefts, it may have contributed to a rise in larceny thefts, which increased by roughly 9 percent (about 135 more thefts per 100,000 residents) compared to other states."[10]

The California Policy Center's Edward Ring noted that "Prop. 47 has led to what police derisively refer to as 'catch and release,' because suspects are only issued citations with a court date and let go. With respect to the homeless, passage of this initiative has made it a waste of time for police to arrest anyone for openly using illegal drugs or for petty theft. Only serious crimes are still investigated. Prop. 47 has enabled anarchy among the homeless and in the neighborhoods where homeless are concentrated."[11]

Furthermore, this increased incidence of theft provides a means for homeless with substance abuse problems to finance their addictions. Beyond the large negative consequences to people's quality of life and the large economic damages, Proposition 47 has helped to trap people in a cycle of addiction, poverty and homelessness – leaving local officials and the courts with limited ability to help get the homeless off the streets.

Policies to More Efficiently Address the Crisis

Sustainably reducing homelessness requires a series of reforms that address each of the drivers of the crisis. These include:

- Making California a more affordable place to live;
- Improving the efficiency of homeless services by empowering nonprofits and better leveraging state resources;
- Repealing harmful policy changes like Prop. 47; and
- Creating homeless courts that are better able to address the issues afflicting this unique population.

Improve California's Affordability

California's unaffordability is the consequence of its policy choices. Making matters worse, there's no evidence demonstrating that the policies driving California's unaffordability are achieving their intended goals. Consequently, California should implement regulatory reforms that lessen these excess costs and, therefore, alleviate the economic pressures driving too many people into homelessness.

Of all necessary reforms, reforming CEQA is arguably the most important because these regulations have become the biggest barrier to homebuilding. Effective reforms will reduce the cost of complying with CEQA regulations and minimize CEQA created time delays by:

- Requiring the plaintiffs in CEQA lawsuits to disclose their economic interests;
- Establishing a more certain CEQA timeline and eliminating duplicative CEQA reviews;
- Eliminating the automatic right of appeal for non-meritorious cases;
- Reducing the timeframe in which claimants can raise issues with respect to an environmental impact report; and
- Codifying a "harmless error" standard that prevents project denials based on minor deficiencies that would likely not impact the approval.

Lessening the onerous zoning regulations would enhance the benefits from CEQA reform. Zoning regulatory reform should simplify the multi-layered restrictions created by planning commissions, zoning adjustment boards and architectural design boards; speed up the housing permit process; and ease restrictions on building duplexes, triplexes, tiny homes and granny flats (smaller second houses on the same lot) in order to expand the stock of affordable housing. Eliminating rent control would also meaningfully expand the housing stock and reduce the costs of housing, particularly in the high-cost cities where housing is the most expensive.

Empower Nonprofits to Improve Homeless Services

Private-sector nonprofits have helped many people transition from the streets into sustainable housing. Many of these private groups have a solid track record of efficiently executing tailored programs for the homeless. Documenting these successes, President Barack Obama acknowledged that, "nonprofits, faith-based and community organizations, and the private and philanthropic sectors are responsible for some of the best thinking, innovation and evidence-based approaches to ending homelessness."[12]

One example is Shelters to Shutters, a nonprofit based in Vienna, Virginia. In partnership with the government, Shelters to Shutters focuses on a holistic approach that emphasizes job placement and housing based on the mantra that "the solution truly needs to be about both."[13] To fulfill this goal, the organization works with apartment management companies "to place people experiencing situational homelessness in onsite, entry-level jobs and provide them with housing at the same communities at which they work."[14]

Another strategy establishes a positive incentive for initiating contact by providing services that many homeless people need. The Crossroads Welcome Center, for instance, is a non-profit organization in Knoxville, Tennessee that provides "a safe place and a starting point for people who are homeless and need a place to stay during the day, as well as a hub where the needy can come and be assessed and get in contact with the correct organizations to help them."[15] The specific services include bag storage, transportation, email and Internet access, and a sitting room. While providing these services, the organization also assesses each client's personal circumstances to determine their needs. According to the University of Tennessee's Mindy Nakamura, "if not for a day room service like this one, there would be an extra 200 people out on the streets every day."[16]

These success stories are not unique. Private-sector institutions have demonstrated greater flexibility and an ability to tailor services to the individual, which creates distinct advantages for these nonprofits over public services. California should avail itself of their expertise by expanding the private sector's role in eliminating homelessness, particularly the people who are homeless due to adverse life or economic events (e.g., the situational homeless).

Compassionate Enforcement

As documented above, not all of the homeless are situational. Many suffer from mental illness and substance abuse issues that prevents them from responding to these types of positive incentives. Based on a policy goal of creating a pathway to recovery, in these instances fulfilling this goal will often require effective negative incentives. Unfortunately, the emerging legal precedents and policy changes discussed above (e.g., Prop. 47) have lessened the ability of the state and local governments to enforce the current laws and provided a means for the homeless suffering from addiction and mental illness to remain on the streets.

Establishing effective negative incentives requires a combination of reforms. Policies that enable the homeless suffering from substance abuse to feed their addictions, such as Prop. 47, need to be repealed. Theft is not only wrong, socially harmful, and economically destructive, it creates a perverse incentive for people struggling with addiction. It enables them to continue engaging in their destructive behavior and discourages them from seeking help. Repealing Prop. 47 would eliminate these perverse incentives. It would also reestablish a punishment for people who violate the law.

However, applying negative incentives is only effective if the interaction is viewed as an opportunity to connect homeless individuals suffering from mental illness or substance abuse problems with the help and resources they need. This can be achieved by establishing homeless courts that have the ability to "sentence" someone to the treatment they need and then expunge their record once their treatment program is successfully completed. In fact, this is the approach of California's Compassionate Intervention Act, a proposed statewide initiative that didn't qualify for the ballot. It did, however, offer a sensible approach.

As its backers explained, the measure "would treat certain existing crimes ... as cries for help – opportunities to both engage the homeless and return respect for the law on our streets. ... under the system, certain crimes, like defecating on public transportation or using heroin or meth in public, would be strictly enforced. However, a special court would be created in major counties to determine whether a person committed those crimes due to economic need, a drug dependency, or mental-health issues. The court would then 'sentence' the defendant to an appropriate treatment plan."

> As supporters further explain, "Unlike other approaches, which have sought to criminalize homelessness itself (too harsh) or have focused purely on the economic aspects of homelessness at the expense of ignoring crimes (too lenient), this initiative seeks a balanced approach.[17]

Adopting a compassionate enforcement approach is an essential part of a comprehensive strategy to address the homeless crisis in California. It supplements the help that private nonprofits provide the homeless who are able to seek help with a means to reach those who are unable to seek help due to mental illness or substance abuse.

Better Leverage State Resources

The state has an important role to play beyond outsourcing the delivery of homeless services to efficient nonprofits and establishing homeless courts. For example, few institutions interact with the homeless population more frequently, and have a better understanding of what is happening on the streets, than law enforcement officers. Law enforcement can become an invaluable resource for addressing the problem by connecting the homeless with the resources that are available to help them. But state and municipal governments need to play a pivotal role making these connections happen.

An example of how these programs could work is the Santa Rosa Homeless Outreach Services Team (HOST), which is operated by Catholic Charities. HOST works with the Santa Rosa Police Department to move unsheltered homeless into services and housing, and to great success.[18] Local pilot programs, based on a long-running program in Eugene, Oregon, would dispatch social workers rather than armed officers to deal with minor disturbances involving homeless people.

Given the severity of the current crisis, transitioning the homeless off the streets is also necessary. Temporary shelter can take many forms. San Diego uses large tents that serve as transitional housing for several hundred clients to fulfill people's immediate shelter needs. San Diego's homeless tent shelters house about 700 people a night and costs roughly $11.3 million a year.[19] It is the type of transitional housing that could help people move off the street immediately. Since transitioning the homeless population into these temporary shelters will mean that fewer funds will be needed for sanitation, temporary tents can be financed by reallocating a city's street-cleaning budget.

As a final role, state and municipal governments have a responsibility to support the nonprofits that are implementing "what works" in as efficient a manner as possible. The deficiencies identified by the state auditor should be corrected such that every dollar is tracked, and its efficacy evaluated properly. The government should judge providers based on their success helping people become self-sufficient members of the community, adjusted for the population being served.

Conclusion

Sustainably addressing California's homelessness crisis is both a moral imperative and an economic necessity. Since homelessness outside of California has been generally declining, California's state and local governments are clearly doing something wrong.

That something includes regulatory policies that price people out of their homes, growing precedents that make it difficult – if not impossible – for the government to enforce the law, and policies that hinder efforts to help the homeless suffering from mental illness or addiction. When coupled with wasteful and inefficient government efforts to address homelessness, California's worst-in-the-nation homeless problem is unsurprising.

California's homeless crisis is the unintended consequence of policies that state and local governments have implemented. While dire, the good news is that since the problem is due to ill-advised policies, it can be reversed by implementing the right ones.

Wayne Winegarden, Ph.D., is a senior fellow in Business & Economics, Pacific Research Institute, as well as the director of PRI's Center for Medical Economics and Innovation.

CHAPTER FOUR: DECONGESTING OUR ROADS AND FREEWAYS

CHAPTER FOUR
DECONGESTING OUR ROADS AND FREEWAYS

By Adrian Moore

*The principal cause of declining freeway development was
the dramatic rise in construction and maintenance costs
during the 1960s, 1970s, and 1980s. Freeway development
costs nationwide grew much faster than the general rate
of inflation during those three decades. Freeway costs rose
faster in California than in the nation as a whole, and faster
in cities than in rural areas.*

—*Brian D. Taylor,*
UCLA professor of urban planning

For a state that prides itself on its economy and being a national leader, California's infrastructure is abysmal. The 2021 infrastructure report card by the American Society of Civil Engineers gives California a C-.[1] That's worse than the C the state received in 2012.

More specifically, they give California a C or C- for the condition of bridges, dams, drinking water, hazardous waste, rail, schools, solid waste, and transit, and a D+, D or D- for storm water, roads, parks, levees, inland waterways and energy. No category in California gets above a C+. Even taking into account that civil engineers make their living off more infrastructure spending, and have an incentive to inflate the problem, they provide a mountain of data and anecdote to back up the terrible state of California's infrastructure.

In a state with earthquakes, you should not have deficient bridges, dams or levees. In a state that prides itself on environmental protection, you should not have deficient storm water, wastewater, hazardous waste or solid waste infrastructure. And you cannot continue to be the fifth-largest economy in the world with deficient roads, schools or drinking water and energy infrastructure.

In the past decade, while California's infrastructure conditions worsened, state spending was exploding. In the last 10 years state spending almost doubled – from about $86 billion to about $164 billion. Yet the state's infrastructure got worse, because the state squanders what it spends, paying too much for everything, pumping billions into foolish and marginal projects, wasting vast sums on overhead and administration, and generally just getting terrible bang for the buck.

In virtually every election, the California Legislature puts one or more infrastructure bond measure up for voter approval. None of it ever seems to improve infrastructure though. Between 1996 and 2006 voters approved $11 billion in water bonds and then between 2006 and 2014 another $11.4 billion dollars for water projects. But by 2018 the Legislature was back asking for another $9 billion, which voters finally, and narrowly, rejected, and meanwhile the condition of state water infrastructure declined.

In 2020, California ranked 43rd on the performance of its state highway system – considering the condition and performance and how much the state spends.[2] Ten years ago it ranked 45th. It has consistently high congestion in the cities, lousy pavement conditions in urban and rural areas, and extraordinarily high administrative costs. Years of high spending and California is still stuck with lousy roads. And since the massive gas tax hike approved in 2017, giving California the highest gas tax in the nation, the roads have not improved one whit.

There is a pattern here. California spends a lot. It spends a lot on infrastructure, but the infrastructure doesn't get better. The spending is not accomplishing any improvements.

Better Infrastructure for California

Infrastructure takes long-term thinking, planning, and prioritizing, and California's poor performance on improving infrastructure shows the lack of all three. California needs to get far more bang for the bucks being spent. It spends seven times as much as Texas per lane mile on administration of highways. Clearly, Texas is focusing on keeping costs down in a way that California is not. This is emblematic of the problem – the money is there; it is being used poorly. Fix that, and the state's infrastructure will improve.

Here are a few ideas to help turn things around.

1. Make infrastructure a priority. The Legislature likes to talk about how important infrastructure is when they put a multibillion-dollar bond measure on the ballot for voters to approve. But they pay little to no attention to how well the money is used, how to get the most out of it, or if their spending is effective. Short-term political issues dominate legislative discussions, not the consistent focus over the years needed to supervise good infrastructure policy. That must change. State policymakers must put infrastructure on the front burner and keep it there for years to ensure the resources spent are yielding results.

2. Prioritize projects based on impact and benefits. Given limited resources, it is vital to steer money to the projects that are the most important and will provide the greatest public benefit. A decade ago, staring at a $59 billion backlog in highway maintenance, state policymakers instead decided to spend what they estimated would be $68 billion on a new bullet train. Roughly $15 billion into that spending, it seems increasingly unlikely the train will ever even connect Merced to Bakersfield, let alone San Francisco to Los Angeles, and meanwhile the highway maintenance backlog has been growing, and road conditions are declining. You can find similar stories in every type of infrastructure in the state. Pet projects, flavors of the day, political imperatives all trump actual benefit for users when it comes to allocating resources.

The Legislature should determine the budget for various infrastructure categories and set policy goals that make clear what criteria agencies should use when determining which projects to do. In any given year, Caltrans should choose from a long list of road maintenance needs and new construction projects to begin. DWR should choose from a long list of water projects. And so on across the various agencies that touch on infrastructure. The policy goals that the Legislature provides should be designed to ensure that the projects with the highest benefits to the most users get built first, taking into account network effects that can multiply the impact of some projects that also make existing infrastructure more useful, such as a road or a water pipeline that allow flow to be shifted between two existing routes.

Each agency responsible for infrastructure should have an Asset Management Plan, a best practice tool in the public and private sector to help meet the desired level of service expected by the users of infrastructure, including needs from projected growth, and determine the strategic use of limited available funding. The plan provides a roadmap for balancing costs, risks and benefits of an infrastructure project across its life cycle. To make this feasible, agencies have to improve their asset management practices, especially high-quality asset inventories that include thorough data on the performance, condition and maintenance schedule for each asset.

Those plans would then flow up to allow the state to create a state capital budget that would evaluate and rank infrastructure projects across all sectors and directs resources to the most important ones. A performance-based infrastructure capital budget aims to allocate the available budget to a subset of investment options that would lead to the maximized total benefits, namely, the largest net gain of positive and negative impacts.

3. Address political and management barriers. For decades, infrastructure stakeholders in California have pointed out that permitting processes seem more designed to deny projects than to approve them. Of course, the permitting process should enforce sensible regulatory requirements, but those should be as clear as possible and the process should be designed to try to find a way to make the project feasible, not try to find reasons to deny it.

Environmental protections can be achieved and a project built – obviously true or no project would ever be approved. But the process needs to be revised to make the goal getting to that balance, to find a way to protect the environment and build needed infrastructure, not to set them up in opposition. And certainly not to fuel the "weaponizing" of environmental laws that we see currently.[3] Environmental and permitting agencies should have the shared goals of the infrastructure agencies to balance the way the Legislature envisions when they set goals and budgets for both. The current environment of conflict, blocking and even lawsuits is the polar opposite of helpful.

Much of the conflict between enforcing environmental protections and building and maintaining infrastructure can be resolved with a few policy changes and a lot of change in management practices by agencies and leadership by the administration. The problem of unions and labor costs is more political than policy. California's prevailing wage requirements for infrastructure projects are specifically designed to drive up labor costs, prevent efforts to use competition to drive down project costs, and thus mean infrastructure projects are more expensive and fewer get built. And state residents and the economy suffer the consequences. The problem is made worse by imposition of Project Labor Agreements, which basically require the builders of a project to reach an agreement with labor unions on labor rules for each project. Since the project can't proceed without the agreement, the unions have all the power in the negotiation, and the result is dramatic increases in project costs and slower projects – to the detriment of the taxpayers and users of the infrastructure.[4]

To date, California state and local governments have chosen policies to benefit the few union workers at the expense of infrastructure projects and the many taxpayers and users of those projects.[5] Frankly, that should be reversed, allowing competitive labor markets to work and that competition to help make infrastructure projects more cost effective.

4. Focus on the long-term life cycle of projects, not just this legislative session. Infrastructure lasts a long time, providing benefits to users for many years. This is why it can make sense to borrow money to build it. In future years, while making payments on the debt, users are also enjoying the benefits of what it built. But this also means that infrastructure projects should be evaluated on a life-cycle basis, which includes risk analysis of events that might cause major rebuild or repair, the regular maintenance costs over the years, and plans for replacement when needed. The idea is to minimize life-cycle costs for infrastructure, not just this budget year's costs. So sometimes building in a more expensive fashion that will reduce maintenance costs makes sense. Sometimes it can be the other way around, especially if technology is driving down maintenance and replacement costs.

This process also discourages deferring maintenance – a problem that plagues California where short-term spending priorities are funded by not maintaining infrastructure and pushing those costs off to the future, when they may be compounded because a simple repair today can become a much more extensive repair if allowed to continue deteriorating. Doing maintenance on schedule and as needed is a proven way to reduce life-cycle costs of infrastructure.

5. Use Public Private Partnerships. States like Texas, Florida and Virginia have seen billions in private capital invested to pay for massive new infrastructure projects through the use of public-private partnerships. Long-term public-private partnerships are contracts between public and private entities for major infrastructure projects that allocate risks between the partners, sparing taxpayers from some major risks, such as cost overruns.

Companies would be thrilled to build airports, sewers, roads and other infrastructure in California. PPPs are a proven tool that, when structured well, can help states get the infrastructure they need without the tax increases and borrowing that California has increasingly relied upon. We know how to properly structure and manage public-private partnerships to protect the taxpayers and ensure accountability. And California clearly has more infrastructure needs than taxpayer dollars can ever fund.

Recent years have seen several success stories for PPPs in California, including the Long Beach Civic Center rebuild, the construction of UC Merced and the Presidio Parkway long-term concession.[6] They have been effective for building new projects and for the maintenance and improvement of existing infrastructure.

Public-private partnerships have several major advantages over traditional project delivery, including:

a. *Delivering needed infrastructure sooner.* P3s can offer a way to finance major infrastructure projects that otherwise might be built years later – or not at all – due to a lack of funding.

b. *Offering the ability to raise large private sources of capital.* Long-term PPPs can raise significant investment capital for new and reconstructed infrastructure because it is attractive to many different types of investors, including public pension funds and insurance companies.

c. *Shifting financial risk from taxpayers to private investors.* PPPs parcel out duties and risks to the parties best able to handle them. The state remains responsible for items like public rights-of-way and environmental permitting. Private companies typically assume the risks associated with construction cost overruns and any possible demand or use fluctuation.

d. *Providing a more business-like approach.* Compared with government agencies, private infrastructure companies tend to be more customer service-oriented and are quicker to adopt cost-saving technologies.

e. *Helping enable major innovations.* The incentive for private partners to innovate, solve difficult problems, and improve service can be a powerful tool. For example, the use of variable-priced tolls to mitigate traffic congestion was pioneered by a private highway operator on State Route 91.

f. *Saving time on project delivery.* On average, new PPP construction is finished ahead of schedule. Compare that to conventional state projects, which take 4 percent to 11 percent longer than scheduled.

g. *Saving money on project delivery.* PPPs can shield government sponsors from cost-overrun risks. Compare that to conventional projects, which on average face 1.5 percent to 13 percent cost overruns.

One form of PPP that has been successful elsewhere, but California has not worked with, is asset recycling. This entails the sale or lease of government owned assets (toll road or bridge, power plant, building, etc.), and using the proceeds to invest in new infrastructure projects. Assets with a user-fee revenue stream most readily lend themselves to this approach. This process not only unlocks the capital value of the assets, which otherwise goes unused by the government, but creates incentives via ownership or lease terms for the private party taking over the asset to invest in upgrades and improvements or make up deferred maintenance.

This type of PPP has been used in Indiana, Illinois, Ohio and Puerto Rico, with great success.[7] For example, Indiana owns a toll road that for years was losing money and accumulating deferred maintenance and obsolete technology. In 2006, they leased that road for 75 years to a private company, getting a $3.8-billion upfront lease payment they used to pay for other needed infrastructure projects for years. At the same time, the state was guaranteed strict requirements for performance of operations of the facility and limitations on toll rate increases. In that part, the arrangement is similar to California's long-term concession of the Presidio Parkway.

Asset recycling can deliver far more than any ordinary form of borrowing could hope to, including interest earnings on the capital value rather than interest payments to a lender, improvements to the asset, performance guarantees for the condition of the asset, and shift of financial risk away from the government.

6. User fees should pay for as much infrastructure as possible. Taxes are subject to political whims and diversion to whatever budget priority a legislature has in any given year. User fees, on the other hand, provide revenue directly tied to how much people are using the infrastructure they pay the fees on.

All infrastructure tends to mostly benefit the ones using it, though there are broader economic benefits as well. User fees that pay for a substantial portion of the infrastructure by charging those that use it makes sense and is more fair and stable than general tax funding, though the latter should make up the balance of the funding on behalf of those broader economic benefits. Infrastructure needs for those with low incomes can be met with the design of the fee structure or with user side subsidies.

Having users pay directly for some or all the cost of infrastructure helps allocate resources to where the user receives the most benefit from them. They also can help reduce or shift demand for infrastructure from congested periods – think roads or parks – and help balance supply as well by showing where more infrastructure is needed if use is overly high, and with revenue from the fees tracking the use.

Benefits of user fee funding of infrastructure include:

Fairness. Those who benefit from the service help to pay for it. And what they pay and what they get for it is relatively transparent.

Choice. User fees give those who pay them much more to the agency of what they pay for, and when and how often they pay it, than do more general taxes. They can make adjustments to lifestyle and location and other choices to improve their benefits from user fee funded systems.

Flexibility. User fees allow system operators the ability to adjust revenues and expenditures, as the economy, demand, and technology change.

Better incentives. User fees create incentives for users to think seriously about the costs of the services they consume and make better decisions about how much to use them – and this is equally true for considering the benefits. At the same time, user fees give system owners and operators better information and incentives to strive for efficiency and quality that keep customers, and revenues, flowing in.

Constraint. If users' costs don't change based on how much they use the system, they have no reason not to over consume it. "Free" roads are a classic example, and congestion, pollution and lost time are the costs paid. User fees internalize those tradeoffs and avoid a "tragedy of the commons" created from broad funding sources that appear "free" to users when making discrete decisions to use the system at a given moment.

California's future depends on infrastructure, pure and simple. A growing population and economy requires food, water, shelter, mobility, recreation and protection from natural disasters. Inadequate infrastructure is a ball and chain on California right now, but some sensible policy changes can turn that around. But it must become a priority and not a second thought, and more important, not something state leaders keep pushing to next year so they can spend more of the budget on ephemeral matters.

Dr. Adrian Moore is vice president of Reason Foundation.

NO FISHING IN MARINA BASIN

CHAPTER FIVE: DEALING WITH DROUGHT

CHAPTER FIVE
DEALING WITH DROUGHT

By Steven Greenhut

*It is easy to forget that the only natural force over which we
have any control out here is water, and that only recently.
In my memory, California summers were characterized
by the coughing in the pipes that meant the well was dry,
and California winters by all-night watches on rivers about
to crest, by sandbagging, by dynamite on the levees and
flooding on the first floor.*

—Joan Didion, author,
from her 1977 essay, 'Holy Water'

California is no stranger to water shortages and even to severe
droughts. The latest one dragged on for six years and dominated
Capitol discussions throughout its tortuous run. The state now is
facing a new one only four years after the last one's completion. California's
go-to approach has been to prod residents into improving their already im-
pressive levels of water conservation, although voters did eventually pass a
water bond that partially funded some water-infrastructure improvements.
The new drought has the potential to be even more severe than the last
one, yet its arrival seems to have taken California policymakers by surprise.

As nearly the entire state faces unusually dry conditions, we're reminded that the governor, Legislature and resource officials took few steps to plan ahead for the inevitable. There's been little commitment to bolstering infrastructure or clearing regulatory hurdles that delay desalination and other water projects.

Gov. Gavin Newsom announced a $5.1-billion package of drought relief measures, but as the *Orange County Register* opined, "That proposal ... deals mainly with short-term mitigation measures.[1] Newsom said the package includes 'bold investments,' but it mostly includes long overdue funds for improving drinking water and wastewater facilities in disadvantaged communities, habitat restoration and land 're-purposing.' These projects are fine, but they will not free us from our crisis-to-crisis approach."

Too often, people look at California's water shortages and say, "Well, that's what you get when you build big cities in the desert." Or, "people simply need to use less water and stop wasting it in swimming pools." In reality, only a small portion of the state is in an actual desert. While California generally is arid, it is not uniformly that way – and swimming pools use only a miniscule percentage of the state's water. Didion is right that they are emblematic of a lifestyle that some people despise – "commonly misapprehended as a trapping of affluence, real or pretended, and of a kind of hedonistic attention to the body." But those pools are literally a drop in the bucket.

California actually receives enough water through rain, snowpack and groundwater to fully meet the needs of its population. Total urban water (residential, commercial, governmental) uses comprise around 10 percent of the state's total water supplies, so taking a conservation-heavy approach only creates diminishing returns – and has a *de minimis* effect on water supplies.[2] If the state's water wars were about numbers – how to store enough water to meet the needs of a specific population – rather than ideology, then California would have met its future needs long ago and water shortages would largely be a non-issue even during droughts.

In fact, it was easy to conclude – based on statements they made during the drought – that some state officials and many environmentalists saw extreme conservation and water rationing as an end in itself. They clearly were using the drought to promote the kind of policies they've always favored and weren't about to let a good crisis go to waste. These activists and leaders didn't seem particularly interested in developing more water supplies, which would mean embracing new water-infrastructure projects and some of the other investments and market-based reforms detailed in my book, *Winning the Water Wars*. They didn't acknowledge that most of the state's water flows out unimpeded to the sea, but typically blamed agricultural and urban users (and Mother Nature) for the shortages. They view water storage, which remains one of the most effective means to plan for future drought years, as a blight.

To their credit, California residents stepped to the plate and achieved stunning water-use reductions by exceeding Gov. Jerry Brown's aggressive conservation goals, but it never seems to be enough for the professional scolds. It's important that we highlight the core problem: a state water policy that is more focused on boosting fish populations and which uses water availability to limit growth and force changes in the way we live. There are various ways to meet the state's water needs. There's too little focus on increasing water supplies (through a variety of projects and approaches) because, frankly, that's not often the goal of those who make public policy. As U.S. Rep. Tom McClintock, R-Roseville, likes to say, "Droughts are nature's fault. They happen. But water shortages are our fault. They are a choice we made when we stopped building adequate storage to meet the needs of the next generation."[3]

California needs an "all of the above" approach to water policy. There are many ways to feed more water into our state's "plumbing" systems. Some are more politically feasible or cost-effective than others, but the goal should be a policy that creates water abundance, through a multiplicity of approaches. In most cases, simply building more surface and groundwater storage facilities is the least costly and most beneficial option – but it's also the one most fraught with political pushback from powerful environmental interests who almost always oppose storage projects, especially through building or expanding dams and reservoirs. We also desperately need more market mechanisms, such as a better means to price water.

Sometimes, projects that are less cost-effective are a reasonable choice because they face fewer political hurdles. When evaluating alternatives, all the costs need to be calculated to choose the best alternative. For instance, the true and total costs of many water-storage projects are hidden (through bonds and taxes). Nevertheless, the end goal should always be adding water into the system. More cost-effective projects always are better than less cost-effective ones, obviously, and they should be funded properly by end users rather than general taxpayers. But water policy always is about compromises.

There's no getting around the power of liberal interest groups to derail sensible water projects. However, conservative water mavens sometimes oppose reasonable projects that add water to the system (desalination) or which fix troublesome water-conveyance issues (the proposed Delta tunnels) because they want to first build more storage. We're dealing with a political world of real-world choices and frustrating obstacles. We shouldn't let the perfect be the enemy of the good. The goal should be abundance – and end-users should, as much as possible, pay for the actual costs of the water.

Sadly, there's a burgeoning movement that wants to decommission some of our existing water-infrastructure systems and move us in the opposite direction – toward a precarious state of scarcity. It's part of a growing nationwide movement to demolish dams and "free" the rivers from their dammed shackles. Some of those policies are driven by a sincere desire to restore wild and scenic rivers (and dam removals sometimes make economic sense), but a lot of it is driven by an ideology that sees humanity as a blight or at least a threat to the state's natural environment. This approach reveals a utopian vision. Many prominent environmentalists envision a rural West that largely is turned back to nature. This is not an exaggeration, nor does it bode well for the future or our state.

We need to face reality. Many environmental groups and their political allies prefer a policy of scarcity, backed by state-imposed limits and edicts, and enforced by inspectors – and they've skillfully refocused (through politics and tireless litigation) the state's water priorities toward these ends. They've derailed many proposed water-infrastructure projects and imposed so many legal and regulatory hurdles on new ones that it often renders them cost-prohibitive or creates decades-long lead times to build them. Many environmental groups function as litigation machines that gear up to stop or slow any water project. (As an aside, Earthjustice's logo is: "Because the Earth needs a good lawyer.") It's just what they do, even if it's not what their good-natured supporters always realize. Yet continuing along this path will further erode Californians' quality of life, undermine the farm economy that feeds the state and the nation, and exacerbate California's highest-in-the-nation poverty rates. These slow-growth, high-price policies are particularly regressive – they harm the poorest people the most by driving up the cost of virtually everything.

Fixing the Problem

To understand how to fix the problem, it's vital to understand how we arrived at our current predicament. State water policy is intertwined with the history of California, so the background – how the state developed its water-rights system and built the giant systems of dams and aqueducts that store and move around our water – says much about who we are as Californians and how our legislative priorities have changed over the years.

The state needs to consider many different proposals and ideas for creating more water supply, from increasing surface storage capacity to building ocean desalination plants to commissioning wastewater recycling facilities. Another important idea is to adopt a more accurate water-pricing system that facilitates water transfers and trading and reduces bad choices and wastefulness that mainly occur when a commodity is available at below its market price (such as growing water-intensive crops such as alfalfa in the Mojave Desert). As always, the marketplace works wonders provided subsidies don't distort the price signals and the government doesn't become too much of an impediment through burdensome or antiquated regulations.

Environmental concerns and fish populations are important, but the state's approach to declining habitats – by basically flushing more water unimpeded through the rivers – has not improved the health of endangered species, especially salmon and Delta smelt. Officials often misdiagnose the problem – or ignore other likely causes for species decline that don't fit their narrative. There are better approaches to helping fish, but almost all of them involve – and here's the term again – a water policy based on *abundance*. California officials can indeed provide more water to help farms, businesses, urban water users and wildlife if they recommit to engineering policies that increase water supplies rather than force us to re-engineer our lives in the face of mandated scarcity. Make no mistake about it, many environmentalists and lawmakers prefer the latter approach.

Putting People First

We need to think about all options and embrace an optimistic way forward that recognizes that human beings, and the farms that feed us, are blessings and not a curse. I strongly endorse conservation, habitat restoration and environmental improvement, but won't apologize for putting people first or for measuring the results – and not just the intentions – of any specific environmental laws and policies.

As you consider water policy, keep the following statistics in mind. California's annual rainfall ranges from 150 million-acre-feet in a dry year to 300 million-acre-feet in a wet one. The California Department of Water Resources says the average is 200 million-acre-feet a year overall. Of that total, 50 percent of the water is diverted for free-flowing environmental uses, 40 percent is used for agriculture and 10 percent is for urban users. Of the latter number, 5.7 percent is for residential uses and 4.3 percent is for commercial, governmental and industrial uses.[4] The raw amounts and percentages vary annually, based on rainfall.

An acre-foot is 326,000 gallons – as much water as it takes to cover an acre of land a foot deep. "An average California household uses between one-half and one acre-foot of water per year for indoor and outdoor use," according to the Water Education Foundation. The average family is using a declining amount of water each year.[5]

Need for More Water Infrastructure

Even though the state's population has doubled since the state and federal governments built any serious water-storage infrastructure in the 1970s, the state's water scarcity can be solved with a few strategies and targeted investments (and ones that cost much less than some of California's other big-ticket and seemingly pointless priorities, such as the $68-billion-plus bullet train). The question is more about priorities and political will than engineering or public finances.

It all comes down to a simple choice: Does the state *want* to build the infrastructure and embrace the other innovations and policies needed to provide us all with plenty of affordable water? Or does it prefer a world of scarcity and skyrocketing prices, where government planners issue rationing edicts and farmers must let vast acreage go fallow?

The problem, ultimately, is a political one: How do we build a consensus for water abundance in a state where the political leadership and so many of the most powerful interest groups are resistant to that concept, or at least – in the case of the Newsom administration – unclear in their goals? I'm not a political activist and have no illusions about how tough it would be to achieve change through the normal process of electioneering – or even by using California's boisterous initiative process. But we can start by changing people's thinking. Here are a few basic talking points for engaging the public:

California's water systems are a triumph of engineering, which have provided Californians with incredible benefits. Those include flood protection, reliable water supplies and recreational opportunities. We shouldn't be ashamed of these accomplishments, which allow us to live productive lives. A few upgrades and improvements to them could significantly increase the amount of usable water.

Many of these major water projects have essentially paid for themselves through revenue bonds, which are repaid by the end users of the water. But the state hasn't built any major water-storage projects since the 1970s, when California's population was roughly half of what it is today. Even the bond measures it passes rarely send significant funding toward surface-storage projects. And in the rare instances they do, as in the case of Sites and Temperance Flat reservoirs, they rarely get built. Completing a number of long-planned water-storage projects is the most cost-effective way to meet our water needs.

The state's water issue isn't about engineering, which is far better today than when the State Water Project, the Central Valley Project and the Colorado River Aqueduct were built. The issue is about our political will. Since that time, California's political focus has shifted heavily toward environmental concerns. Those concerns are important, but often are used as a pre-text to promote growth control and other dubious agendas.

As environmentalists like to say, the state is locked into "binaries" that endlessly pit fish against people. Unfortunately, those same environmentalists are typically opposed to new water-infrastructure projects and regulatory reforms, which would help put an end to that construct by feeding significant amounts of water into our plumbing systems.

The environmental preference for flushing more water through our rivers and out to the sea has not led to the restoration of fish populations. Some of the endangered fish, such as the Delta smelt, have been impacted more by poorly treated urban wastewater and invasive species (predators such as striped bass) than by water diversions for farmers.

Most environmental groups are habitually opposed to any project that yields more water supply, including seemingly unobjectionable desalination plants and other privately funded projects such as the Cadiz water project in the Mojave Desert.

This opposition tends to be ideological and often is about stopping growth. Yet, without water infrastructure California would largely be a wasteland or at least largely uninhabited. There's nothing wrong with prioritizing the needs of people, while still paying attention to habitat restoration. More water allows us to deal with all these priorities.

The state allows half of its annual water to flow unimpeded to the sea. Our goal should be to store more water in wet years so that there's plenty to go around during frequent drought years. The question is one of goals: Do we want scarcity or abundance?

If California continues along the path of scarcity, then it will ultimately lead to more government mandates. Californians have made remarkable progress in conserving water, but urban uses comprise a small percentage of the total water use that flows through our state, so we can quickly reach a point of diminishing returns.

Desalination, Water Recycling and Innovation

In addition to building more surface and groundwater storage facilities, California can deal with its water problems by building ocean desalination plants and increasing its commitment to wastewater reuse and other innovations. The question comes down to costs v. benefits for each particular proposal, but our approach ought to be laser-focused on feeding more water into the system. Water recycling, in particular, is cost-effective and unobjectionable.

Bolstering Water Rights, Trading and Pricing

The state needs to reform its regulatory barriers to water trading, so water-rights holders are better able to sell water to those who need it most. We also need a better pricing system to allow markets to work their magic. But pricing must come against a backdrop of water abundance rather than one that leaves everyone fighting over an artificially capped supply. The state also lacks an accurate means of pricing water, which is bizarre in a state as tech-savvy as ours.

Fixing the Delta Conveyance System

California needs to fix the conveyance system through the Sacramento-San Joaquin Valley, which now is the equivalent of a six-lane highway that feeds into a series of dirt roads. The tangle there impedes flows and has led to the erosion of the region's ecosystem. The Delta tunnel(s) project isn't ostensibly designed to send more water southward, but to provide more reliable water flows that aren't halted when endangered fish are found near the water pumps at Tracy. At some point, California needs to fix this conveyance system, through the tunnel project or something similar.

As the near-crisis at Oroville Dam showed, California has not adequately maintained its existing water infrastructure – just as it has neglected its transportation infrastructure. It's another reminder that the water issue is mostly about the state's spending priorities.

The San Joaquin Valley is the world's agricultural breadbasket. Restrictions on pumping endanger not only the economy of the state's Central Valley, but the abundance of food products we take for granted. There's a need to measure and control groundwater pumping, but policymakers need to figure out a way to get water to farm regions that are reliant on groundwater pumping.

In 2020, the Newsom administration released its compromise plan that, as the governor said, is "a path forward, one that will move past the old water binaries and set us up for a secure and prosperous water future." The deal, as *CalMatters*' Dan Walters reported, "would enhance flows through the Delta by up to 900,000 acre-feet a year and restore 60,000 acres of habitat for wildlife, particularly salmon."[6] His column asked, "Has Newsom settled the water wars?" The answer would seem to be a resounding "no" – especially after the administration announced a lawsuit to stop the Trump administration's decision to send more federally controlled water to farmers in the valley.

The Newsom plan is reasonable enough, but it doesn't do the one thing California needs most: significantly improve the state's water infrastructure and plan for a future of abundance. Capturing more water is the key to a vibrant future. At this writing, the usual binaries are playing out – and in a more heated fashion than usual. So, no, California is not making any progress.

Changing Our Attitude About Water

I'll conclude with two quotations that epitomize the choice Californians face going forward.

The first is from Wallace Stegner, the late environmentalist writer, who epitomized the common narrative about water and the growing western states: "We may love a place and still be dangerous to it. We have tried to make the arid west what it was never meant to be and cannot remain, the Garden of the World and the home of multiple millions."[7] Like other environmentalist writers, Stegner saw the main problem as one of mankind settling in a place that should largely been left unsettled. I reject that conclusion.

The second is from the 1957 *California Water Plan*. The state has changed dramatically in the ensuing 63 years, but the question about our future remains largely the same as it was then:

> Today, the future agricultural, urban, and industrial growth of California hinges on a highly important decision, which is well within the power of the people to make. We can move forward with a thriving economy by pursuing a vigorous and progressive water development planning and construction program; or we can allow our economy to stagnate, perhaps even retrogress, by adopting a complacent attitude and leaving each district, community, agency, or other entity to secure its own water supply as best it can with small regard to the needs of others.[8]

Californians can select a dismal world of scarcity, higher prices, fewer lifestyle choices and less economic opportunity as part of a myopic desire to return our region to its less-populated past. Or we can choose to build the water-storage facilities, reform the water-pricing system, reduce regulations that impede innovation, embrace water recycling, desalination and other ideas and assure a bright future of abundance, freedom and growth.

Steven Greenhut is Western region director for the R Street Institute, a member of the Southern California News Group editorial board and author of the Pacific Research Institute book, Winning the Water Wars, *from which this chapter is excerpted.*

CHAPTER SIX: A RETURN TO EDUCATIONAL EXCELLENCE

CHAPTER SIX
A RETURN TO EDUCATIONAL EXCELLENCE

By Lance Izumi

*Perhaps the most important of these general principles is
that schools exist for the education of children. Schools
do not exist to provide iron-clad jobs for teachers, billions
of dollars in union dues for teachers unions, monopolies
for educational bureaucracies, a guaranteed market
for teachers college degrees or a captive audience for
indoctrinators.*

—Thomas Sowell

California may be a leader in many areas, but K-12 public education is certainly not one of them. For years, the state's public school system has been marked by poor-performing students and outsized influence of special interests such as teachers unions.

Even before the COVID-19 pandemic, too many of California's public school students were achieving at low levels according to various state and national tests.

The California Assessment of Student Performance and Progress (CAASPP), which is the state-administered exam given to public school students in grades three to eight and in grade 11, tests students in English language arts and mathematics and grades students according to whether they meet grade-level standards.

For the 2018-19 school year, the overall CAASPP results were troubling. On the CAASPP English exam, 49 percent of California students tested, about half, failed to meet grade-level standards. On the CAASPP math exam, 60 percent of the state students tested failed to meet grade-level standards.[1]

As bad as these achievement statistics are, the news is even worse when one looks at the performance of students from various subgroups.

Among low-income students tested, 61 percent failed to meet grade-level standards in English, while 73 percent failed to meet grade level standards in math.[2]

For Latino students, 59 percent failed to meet grade-level standards in English and 72 percent failed to meet grade-level standards in math.[3]

Among African-American students tested, 67 percent failed to meet grade-level standards in English and 79 percent failed to meet grade-level standards in math.[4]

These abysmal achievement levels are not limited to results on the state's exam. The National Assessment of Educational Progress (NAEP), which is often referred to as the nation's report card, is administered in almost all states, including California. NAEP tests a representative sample of students in each state in reading and math in grades four and eight.

On the eighth-grade NAEP exam in reading, 70 percent of California students tested failed to perform at the proficient level on the exam. Among low-income students, 82 percent failed to achieve at proficiency. Even among non-low-income students, 53 percent failed to perform at the proficient mark.[5]

Among Latino eighth-graders, 81 percent failed to achieve at the proficient level on the NAEP reading test, while 90 percent of African-American eighth-graders failed to hit the proficient mark.[6]

Results were just as bad on the eighth-grade NAEP math exam. Seventy-one percent of California student test-takers failed to perform at the proficient level. Among low-income students, 84 percent failed to achieve proficiency, while half of non-low-income students failed to make the proficient level.[7]

Among Latino eighth-graders, 85 percent failed to achieve at the proficient level on the NAEP math test, while 90 percent of African-American eighth-graders failed to hit proficiency.[8]

Remember, all these poor performance results were before COVID-19 shut down California's public schools, which has caused student learning to suffer even more. Indeed, data are now showing significant learning losses among students since the public school closures.

One of the first comprehensive studies on the state of student learning in California in the COVID-19 era was released in January 2021 by the research organization PACE, which is sponsored by the University of California at Los Angeles, the University of Southern California, the University of California Davis, Stanford University, and the University of California, Berkeley.

The PACE study examined 18 school districts across California and analyzed English and math test scores of students.[9]

The study found that there was significant learning loss in both English and math in the early grades among students, which is concerning since early learning is the foundation for later educational success.[10]

Given that California has a high proportion of students who come from low-income family backgrounds, it is especially troubling that school closures have had a disproportionate impact on low-income children.

According to the study, there was significantly more learning loss from Fall 2019 to Fall 2020 compared to previous years for students from socioeconomically disadvantaged backgrounds, particularly in English.[11]

Further, given the high proportion of non-English-fluent children in California, it is also very troubling to see large learning losses among these English-language-learner students as well.

These non-English-fluent children lost learning in English in nearly every grade and in the early grades in math. The loss was particularly severe in some grades.[12]

For example, in the fifth grade, non-English-fluent children lost roughly 30 percent of a year in typical growth in English performance.[13]

The PACE study said that the poor performance of non-English-fluent children are "likely due to the substantial challenges with supporting students who are learning English in a virtual setting."[14]

The study authors concluded: "Average learning loss estimates mask the reality that some students in California are suffering much more during this time than others. Without aggressive and bold actions, these students may never catch up."[15]

Another indicator of students experiencing learning loss is the increase in failing grades. For example, according to data from the Los Angeles Unified School District, the number of failing grades has increased significantly during the pandemic.

So, if students are learning so little, then what is one of the things one would also expect to see as a consequence? Answer: lower enrollment because students either drop out or take advantage of another education option.

Students who are not learning get frustrated, so they do not see why they should stay in school when they cannot actually go to school and learn. California is seeing a huge wave of what amounts to students voting with their feet to leave the regular public schools.

According to state data released in January 2021, California has experienced a record one-year enrollment nosedive of 155,000 students. For comparison, that drop-off is more than five times greater than California's usual annual rate of enrollment decline.[16] Los Angeles Unified saw an enrollment drop of 6,000 students in kindergarten alone, which is a 14 percent decline over the previous year.[17]

The Charter School Option

So, amidst all this bad news in the regular public school system, is there any better alternative? One ready option is the state's charter school sector.

Charter schools are publicly funded schools that are independent of school districts with greater autonomy to innovate. Various indicators show that charter school students, especially Latinos and African Americans achieve at higher levels than their peers in the regular public schools.[18]

Thus, on average, on the CAASPP exam, Latino and African American charter school students are closer to reaching grade-level standards than their regular public school peers. African American charter school students outperform their district school peers in both English and math, while Latino charter school students outperform their district peers in English and are on par in math.[19]

In Los Angeles, charter schools performed better than Los Angeles Unified School District schools on the CAASPP math and English exams across every measured student subgroup. Similar results can be seen in other cities such as Oakland.[20]

Further, as the California Charter School Association noted, "charter schools had higher rates of UC/CSU enrollment with all subgroups" than regular public schools in 2018, and were "especially successful at getting black, Latinx, and low-income students into these universities."[21]

Many charter schools have followed the scientific evidence and remained open during the COVID-19 pandemic, which has allowed their students to avoid the learning losses that regular public school students have suffered.

It has been three decades since California enacted legislation that established charter schools. Today, there are more than 1,300 charter schools in the state serving 675,000 students.[22] Realistically, the only public alternative to the regular public schools is the charter school sector. Perversely, because charter schools have been one of California education's few bright spots, they are facing attacks on multiple fronts.

Charter schools are largely non-union, which is why they can be so flexible and innovative, so teachers unions have used strikes to call for caps on new charter schools. They have also used the COVID-19 pandemic to push against charters. And they have used their overwhelming influence in the State Capitol to enact an array of anti-charter measures.

The 'Drain the Public Schools' Myth

Before examining Sacramento's legislative assault against charter schools, it is important to dispel one of the most pernicious myths about charter schools, which is that that they "drain" funding away from regular public schools. Teachers unions have used this "draining" claim as one of their primary arguments in their continuing war against charter schools.

For example, in 2019, as state lawmakers debated anti-charter-school legislation, then-California Teachers Association president Eric Heins claimed that charter schools are "a drain on many of our public schools."[23] The claim that charter schools drain funding away from regular public schools is a popular union talking point, but it is also demonstrably false.

A series of studies from the Center on Reinventing Public Education at the University of Washington Bothell specifically analyzed the financial impact of California's charter schools on the state's regular public school system since "critics in California and nationwide have claimed charter school growth undermines school district finances and forces cuts in the quality of schooling districts can provide."[24]

The researchers' findings tell a much different story than the claims of union leaders and other charter-school opponents. For instance, the growth of charter schools has had little impact on the financial distress of school districts:

Charter schools have grown at an average clip of 0.5 percent a year since 1998. If growing charter school enrollments financially stress school districts, we would expect an escalating pattern of fiscal distress – with school districts entering distress and remaining there as the charter sector continues to enroll more students. The reality looks considerably different.

Of the nearly 1,000 school districts in the state, just a handful have ever entered fiscal distress. The number of districts in fiscal distress has evolved over time, increasing during recessionary periods and decreasing during expansionary periods. Despite all-time high enrollment in charter schools, just four school districts were in fiscal distress in the 2018-2019 school year. This compares to an all-time high of 16 districts in 2009-2010, during the Great Recession.[25]

Thus, said the researchers, "enrollment loss to charter schools is not closely connected to fiscal distress among California school districts."[26] In other words, the regular public school system should learn from the competition, not destroy it.

So, what do we know about California charter schools?

We know that they do not cause the regular public schools to enter financial distress due to draining away funding. We know that charter schools often receive much less public and non-public funding than regular public schools. And we know that among various student-achievement indicators, charter schools outperform regular public schools.

Charter schools are therefore a successful bargain in education. Yet, state lawmakers, at the behest of the teachers unions, have targeted charter schools.

Sacramento's Attack on Charter Schools

The National Alliance of Public Charter Schools (NAPCS) has put together model legislation, which contains 21 components that it deems essential for a good charter-school law. These elements include:

- No caps on the growth of charter schools
- A variety of charter schools allowed
- Authorizer and overall program accountability system required
- Adequate authorizer funding
- Transparent charter school application, review, and decision-making processes
- Performance-based charter school contracts required
- Comprehensive charter school monitoring and data collection
- Clear processes for renewal, nonrenewal and revocation
- Transparency regarding educational service providers
- Fiscally and legally autonomous schools with independent charter school boards
- Clear student enrollment and lottery procedures
- Automatic exemptions from many state and district laws and regulations

- Automatic collective bargaining exemption
- Multi-school charter contract and/or multi-charter school contract boards allowed
- Extracurricular and interscholastic activities eligibility and access
- Clear identification of special education responsibilities
- Equitable operational funding and equal access to all state and federal categorical funding
- Equitable access to capital funding and facilities
- Access to relevant employee retirement systems
- Full-time virtual charter school provisions[27]

For many years, California was viewed as having one of the better state charter-school laws, meeting many of NAPCS' requirements. Further, California governors of both parties have been supportive of charter schools and defended them against attacks from teachers unions and their allies in the Legislature. That all changed when Gavin Newsom became governor.

Nina Rees, NAPCS president, and Todd Ziebarth, NAPCS senior vice president, noted, "instead of having supportive Governor Jerry Brown in California, charter school advocates had to deal with Democratic Governor Gavin Newsom, hardly the supporter Brown was."[28] Such a political change had immediate negative consequences for charter schools.

NAPCS noted that California's ranking fell from the 18th to the 20th position "because it weakened the state's appellate process and eliminated teacher certification flexibility for charter schools."[29] California's rank fell even more precipitously in other ranking systems.[30] Yet, the NAPCS down-ranking of California does not tell the whole story of the state's recent undermining of charter schools.

Under Assembly Bill 1505, which was signed into law by Newsom in 2019, local school boards can deny a charter petition if it finds that the proposed charter "is demonstrably unlikely to serve the interests of the entire community," which is a carte-blanche reason to deny any charter petition.[31]

This anti-community-interests provision requires the inclusion of "considerations of the fiscal impact of the proposed charter school."[32] Of course, despite the research showing that charter schools do not cause the financial distress of school districts, every school board will claim that charters adversely impact the district bottom line, making budgetary mountains out of tiny charter molehills.

Also, proposed charter schools can be denied if they "would substantially undermine existing services, academic offerings, or programmatic offerings," an excuse big enough for school boards to run a train through.[33]

In addition, school boards can disapprove proposed charters if they "duplicate a program currently offered within the school district," with nothing said about whether the district is effectively providing the duplicated program.[34]

Further, in districts that have been judged as being unlikely to meet their financial obligations, a rebuttable presumption of denial of a charter petition will now be the standard, which Newsom's office interprets to mean, "The presumption in those districts will be that new charters will not open."[35] So children in badly mismanaged school districts will be forced to attend inefficient and ineffective regular public schools, which perversely rewards the mismanagement of those poorly run districts.

Remember, too, that the anti-charter legislation signed by Newsom was the direct result of the strikes by the teachers' unions in Los Angeles and Oakland in 2019.

EdSource, the respected California education publication, pointed out that union leaders "believe that labor conflicts played a role in forcing the hand of legislative leaders – including Gov. Newsom" to change California's charter law to "allow districts, like Oakland and Los Angeles, to take into account the financial impact of a charter school on the district when deciding whether to allow it to open."[36] Giving school districts vague open-ended excuses to turn down proposals for new charter schools effectively stops any new charter from being established.

In the midst of the COVID crisis, California lawmakers changed charter-school funding rules for growing charter schools. The state will fund higher enrollment at charter schools based on either the projected number of students in the schools' own 2020-21 budgets or on their enrollment figures as of October 1st, but whichever figure is lower.[37]

To understand the impact of this new stipulation, one can imagine a charter school that projects 400 new students in its 2020-21 budget. However, on Oct. 1, the school has 500 new students. According to the funding rule, the state will not pay for the added 100 students as of Oct. 1 because the projected number of students in the school's budget was the lower amount vis-à-vis the actual number of students that eventually enrolled.

By failing to fund every student, California lawmakers went against state court rulings requiring equal treatment for all students and state education reform laws that guarantee that funding must follow a child to the child's new school.[38]

What Policymakers Should Do

Given the generally terrible state of California's regular public school system, what should lawmakers and other policymakers do? Here are six top recommendations:

- Regular public schools should emulate charter schools and reopen in fall 2021 to full five-day-a-week in-person instruction.

- Anti-charter-school laws such as AB 1505 should be repealed.

- Alert Californians to new anti-charter-school bills that are making their way through the Legislature.

- Offer a positive pro-charter-school agenda based on the model legislation proposed by organizations such as the National Alliance of Public Charter Schools.

- Support efforts to encourage teachers to opt out of their unions.

- Finally, policymakers should look beyond charter schools to other school choice tools such as education savings accounts. Other states are implementing such choice programs and California's leaders should learn from their example.

Regarding the first recommendation, studies by the Centers for Disease Control and others have shown that there is very little transmission of COVID-19 in schools.[39] Many charter schools have successfully stayed open to full in-person instruction during the pandemic.

For example, John Adams Academy charter school, which has three campuses outside of Sacramento, has been open to five-day-a-week in-person instruction since fall. Students were given the option of choosing in-person instruction or learning remotely. The vast majority opted for in-person learning.

To ensure safety, students are placed in a cohort. If anyone in the cohort is exposed to COVID then the cohort is quarantined. During the 2020-21 school year, John Adams used protocols such as mask wearing, social distancing, and one-way corridors. According to school officials, there was not a single case of in-school transmission of COVID on any of the campuses.

The second recommendation naturally follows from the legislative actions described in the previous section. Yet, the opponents of charter schools will never rest until they destroy the charter school sector, which is why recommendation three is important.

In 2021, a particularly egregious bill, Assembly Bill 1316, was making its way through the Legislature. According to Sacramento County Board of Education member Paul Keefer:

> Specifically, the bill limits school choice by prohibiting parents and students from choosing a public charter school outside the county in which they reside. It also caps enrollment at non-classroom based public charter schools when they are authorized by a small school district whose average daily attendance is 10,000 students or less.

These negative impacts are occurring while thousands of students remain unaccounted for in our traditional school districts due to the COVID pandemic. Keefer rightly concludes: "I'm afraid this bill – and other legislative attacks – are all about politics and power. Otherwise, why would policymakers so blatantly be picking winners and losers among public school students during the worst pandemic in 100 years?"[40] The measure was pulled by its author, Assembly Education Committee chairman Patrick O'Donnell, D-Long Beach, in June 2021. While successful in this case, lawmakers must remain vigilant in fighting against these new assaults against charter schools.

It is not enough, however, to fight flawed laws and legislative proposals. It is important to present a positive alternative to bad ideas. The National Alliance of Public Charter Schools, for instance, maintains a charter law database that helps lawmakers "write laws that encourage the creation and growth of high-quality charter schools."[41]

Recommendation number five goes to the heart of the beast, so to speak. As has been pointed out in this chapter, the California Teachers' Association and the various local teachers' unions in California have been implacable foes of charter schools. They have also been the barrier to implementing real education reforms and the catalyst for much bad public education policy generally.

While the CTA is the highest spending lobby in Sacramento, many rank-and-file teachers do not support all the positions of the union. And since teachers now have the ability, due to court decisions, to opt out of paying union dues and fees, reform-minded lawmakers and policymakers should ensure all public employees are fully educated about their newly won worker freedom rights.

Finally, while the discussion so far has been about charter schools as an alternative to the regular public schools, California policymakers should understand that other states are adopting other school choice options for parents to utilize.

For example, West Virginia, which like California suffers from poor-performing public schools, recently enacted the nation's most expansive education savings account (ESA) program, which will create savings accounts for parents of students leaving the public school system to use 100 percent of state education dollars, or about $4,600 per year, to pay for private school tuition, homeschool curriculum, and other learning expenses.[42]

Under the provisions of the West Virginia ESA law, every child in a public school is eligible for an ESA, which means an amazing 90 percent of the state's students will be able to use the ESAs.

The enactment of the West Virginia ESA law came on the heels of a new Georgia Public Policy Foundation study showing that ESAs would result in "higher lifetime earnings associated with increases in academic achievement," large economic benefits to the state, and tax savings from reduced social costs such as crime.[43]

The study's author Corey DeAngelis, national director of research at the American Federation for Children, points out, "Funding students, as opposed to systems, would benefit families by empowering them to choose the education provider that best meets their needs—public or private, in-person or remote."[44]

For California lawmakers and policymakers, therefore, there are two main fights. First, the battle to protect the gains achieved through the state's charter school sector. Second, to think big and advocate for those types of school choice options that may not seem immediately do-able in California, but which other states are now implementing. If reform-minded policymakers do not start building the foundation of public support for these more expansive school choice options through effective advocacy, then nothing better for California parents can happen in coming years.

We must not pine away for some imagined past golden era of California education, but, rather, we must build the future of education we want to see for all our children.

Lance Izumi is senior director of the Center for Education at the Pacific Research Institute. He has written and produced books, studies and films on a wide variety of education topics. Most recently, he is the author of the 2017 book The Corrupt Classroom *and the 2019 book* Choosing Diversity: How Charter Schools Promote Diverse Learning Models and Meet the Diverse Needs of Parents and Children.

CHAPTER SEVEN: ARRESTING CALIFORNIA'S CRIME PROBLEM

CHAPTER SEVEN
ARRESTING CALIFORNIA'S CRIME PROBLEM

By Pat Nolan

As with any government program, the criminal justice system must be transparent and include performance measures that hold it accountable for its results in protecting the public, lowering crime rates, reducing re-offending, collecting victim restitution and conserving taxpayers' money.

—Right on Crime,
statement of principles

The first responsibility of government is keeping the public safe from harm within the constraints of individual liberty and limited government. By all measures, it is clear that California's government is failing to protect its people.

After 25 years of declining crime rates, 2021 finds Californians suffering from a crime wave that is terrorizing rural and urban communities alike.

Here are some of the stunning facts:

- The number of homicide victims in California jumped 27 percent from 2019 to 2020,[1] to about 2,300, marking the largest year-over-year increase in three decades. There were 5.8 homicides per 100,000 residents in 2020, the highest rate in California since 2008.

- And the number has risen much higher in 2021. Homicides increased by a whopping 40 percent in Los Angeles, 36 percent in Oakland, 17 percent in San Francisco, and 10 percent in San Diego. [2]

- Car thefts in California jumped 24 percent. Commercial burglaries rose by about 26 percent. San Francisco saw a startling 78 percent increase in residential burglaries.[3]

What is driving this dramatic increase in violent crime? Some blame the pandemic for the rise in crime. But a little research proves that is simply not true. Other nations whose economies suffered far more than the United States experienced drops in crime. For example:

- The murder rate fell in London by 16 percent in 2020, even though England suffered far more economic harm than did America.[4]

- Italy was hit hard and early by the pandemic. Yet, murders fell by 14 percent, from 315 to 271.[5]

- France, despite the roiling street protests in Paris, saw murders drop by 2 percent to 863.

- Japan experienced the lowest murder rate since World War II.[6]

- In Mexico, murders declined for the first time in six years – despite the increased activities of the cartels.[7]

Others say that we need longer sentences to dissuade criminals from a life of crime and encourage them to find another line of work. Yet, California has some of the longest sentences in the nation. That hasn't stemmed the meteoric rise in crime. Criminals are not rational calculators. I have never met an inmate that thought he would be caught. And none of them had the foggiest idea what the penalty for their crime was at the time they committed it.

Which prompts the question: Are California residents more immoral or dangerous than people in other states? I don't think so. Rather it is the way the state handles violent crime that is badly off track.

'Woke' Prosecutors Endanger Residents

It is hard to fight crime when part of the team believes that society is to blame for violence rather than the person who harmed an innocent person. San Francisco and Los Angeles have elected the most radical prosecutors in the history of our state, Chesa Boudin and George Gascón respectively. On taking office, each announced a long list of crimes they will no longer prosecute. What arrogance. In doing this, they usurped the constitutional role of the Legislature in deciding what is a crime and what isn't.

How did such "progressive prosecutors" win these important posts? George Soros and his coterie of billionaire friends from the Bay Area poured millions into their races overwhelming the meager resources of the more traditional prosecutors they ousted.

At Boudin's victory party his supporters chanted "F*ck the POA (Police Officers Association)."[8] In Los Angeles, Gascón immediately disbanded the gang prosecution unit. It seems that despite the evidence to the contrary Gascón believes gangs are not the problem in the streets of his city. Gascón says we need gun control to stop the bloodshed. How silly. As if the gangs will stop using guns to eliminate their competitors.

These purported "protectors of the rule of law" are actually its enemies, waging war from the inside. In fact, one of their fellow radical district attorneys, Larry Krasner of Philadelphia, refers to himself as a "public defender with power."[9] That's an odd way for a prosecutor to view his role.

It is particularly painful for me to see these charlatans masquerade as criminal justice reformers. I have worked to reform the justice system for the last 25 years. I was instrumental in the passage of the Prison Rape Elimination Act, the Fair Sentencing Act, the Second Chance Act, and the First Step Act. I know a phony when I see one, and these "woke" prosecutors are as bogus as that Rolex watch you bought from a street vendor on the streets of New York.

As *Reason* magazine has written, "it's so important to distinguish between worthwhile criminal justice reform and simply failing to enforce the rule of law." For California to get a grip on crime, prosecutors must understand that some people are so dangerous that they need to be isolated from the rest of us. They must understand that while social workers are sometimes needed, they don't do much good in a shootout.

The California Department of Corrections and Rehabilitation Is Badly Broken

California runs 34 prisons which hold 120,000 inmates at an annual cost to taxpayers of $16 billion.[10] Yet, many Californians – particularly the elderly, the poor, and the young – cower behind bars, afraid of becoming the next victim of crime.

You'd think being sent to prison once would be enough. Yet more than half of released inmates return to prison within three years.[11] That is a failure rate of 50 percent. No other business would continue to operate with a failure rate of 50 percent. That is a terrible return for our investment.

Only a state that is rich and foolish would continue to pour billions into a system that releases prisoners just as dangerous as when they entered, ignores the needs of victims, and leaves its communities living in fear of crime. Too be blunt, California is not getting enough public safety for the billions it spends on the justice system.

How can the state reverse the increase in crime? I am a conservative, and we have a responsibility to lead the way out of the current mess. We know it is the nature of bureaucracy that government agencies grow in size and inefficiency. The justice system must be held accountable for wise use of tax dollars just as it holds offenders accountable for their actions.

Here are some concrete suggestions for making Californians safer:

REPAIR THE HARM DONE TO VICTIMS

Crime is more than lawbreaking – it is victim harming. Victims should be involved at all stages of the justice process, and the system should hold offenders accountable to repair the harm they did to the victim. To be meaningful, restitution should be paid directly to the offender by the offender. That is how the Bible describes restitution, "(H)e shall make full restitution for his wrong, adding a fifth to it and giving it to him to whom he did the wrong."

Unfortunately, that is not the way California handles "restitution." Currently, all inmates are fined a flat amount, and the money put in the victims' fund. The victim does not receive the payment from the person who harmed them, and the payment bears no relation to the magnitude of the harm they suffered. Instead, the money is parsed out by the impersonal bureaucracy with photo ops for the attorney general. This is a system designed by politicians for the benefit of politicians.

WE NEED PRISONS TO PROTECT SOCIETY FROM VIOLENT OFFENDERS

Some "reformers" actually want to abolish prisons. That is just plain silly. Of course, we need prisons to isolate offenders who threaten the safety of the community. But if we want to reduce crime, we must try to lower the recidivism rate.

Over 95 percent of these dangerous inmates will eventually end their sentences and be released.[12] We must do all we can prepare them to be good neighbors. Certainly, some cannot desist from a life of crime. However, California only pays lip service to helping them turn over a new leaf.

INMATES WITH ADDICTIONS NEED ACCESS TO TREATMENT PROGRAMS

We must increase treatment for drug and alcohol addiction. Over 80 percent of inmates are addicted to drugs or alcohol, but less than 20 percent of inmates receive treatment for their addiction.[13] Locking up addicts while doing nothing to help them overcome their addiction is a fraud on the public.

By the way, don't buy into the line that "at least they won't do drugs in prisons." Drugs of all kinds are freely available inside our jails and prisons. And not all of the drugs enter through visitation. Why do you think the corrections officers so strenuously object to having their lunch buckets checked on entering the prisons?[14]

DON'T LOCK UP THE NON-DANGEROUS MENTALLY ILL; THEY ARE SICK - NOT BAD

Treat the non-dangerous mentally ill in community facilities rather than in jails and prisons. At least 25 percent of inmates suffer from a mental illness.[15] Of course, some people with mental illness are very dangerous. But thousands are merely sick and pose no threat. They end up in our jails and prisons as a result of "mercy bookings." The police would much rather take them to a civilian facility for proper treatment, but few beds are available. Holding the mentally ill behind bars is very costly. Taxpayers spend $65 a day to jail the mentally ill; community treatment costs only $29. Money spent on new community mental health facilities would be far cheaper than building more prisons.

Most prisoners are placed in prisons several hours from their homes, making family visits almost impossible. In addition, many prison policies make it difficult for families to remain in contact. Yet, studies show that an intact family is the greatest positive factor in ensuring a successful transition from prison to the community. Prisons should establish policies and programs that strengthen families and encourage frequent contact with them.

Several police departments have created programs to divert people with drug and mental health issues out of the criminal justice system and into the treatment they need. Seattle instituted the Law Enforcement Assisted Diversion ("LEAD") program, which encourages officers to bring low-level drug arrestees to treatment rather than booking.[16] LEAD participants are 58 percent less likely to be rearrested compared to those arrested and booked. Similarly, Miami-Dade County provides training for police officers to better prepare them to help people experiencing serious mental health issues. The average daily jail population decreased 38 percent as a result.

PRISONS SHOULD PREPARE INMATES TO BE GOOD NEIGHBORS ON RELEASE

Prisons should do more than warehouse inmates. Most prisoners are idle much of the day, with few programs available to prepare them to stay on the straight and narrow after release. Instead, our prisons should prepare offenders for their return to society by providing GED classes, anger management, how to be a good parent and marketable job skills. The cost of these programs is far exceeded by the savings from the resulting drop in crime rates. Helping prisoners get back on their feet after they finish their sentences is a matter of public safety as well as a means of saving taxpayer money – and it will result in fewer victims. We just can't afford to have offenders cycling in and out of prison.

Yet, as important as preparing inmates for return is, California does a terrible job providing such essential programs. A damning report from California's State Auditor[17] included these findings:

- Corrections has neither consistently placed inmates on waiting lists for needed rehabilitation programs nor prioritized those with the highest need correctly.
- Corrections failed to meet any of the rehabilitative needs for 62 percent of the inmates who had been assessed as at risk to recidivate.
- Corrections does not have ANY performance measures for its rehabilitation programs, such as a target reduction in recidivism, nor an assessment of the cost-effectiveness of the few programs they do provide.

PRISONERS SHOULD HAVE ACCESS TO FAITH-BASED PROGRAMS

You would think prison officials would do all they can to allow inmates to participate in religious activities. Even an atheist warden would acknowledge the positive impact faith programs have on inmates. If you were a corrections officer being approached by a group of inmates, would it make a difference if you knew they were coming from a Bible study? Of course it would. Yet, many prisons make it difficult for religious volunteers to work with inmates.

It is not because these prison officers have an animus to religion. Rather, they don't want to do the extra work to clear volunteers into prisons. It is easier to turn them away than it is to do the paperwork. In one instance, the officer on duty told the volunteers that they weren't on the "approved list" even though they had been coming to that prison for over two years.

The truth is that the officer had been playing a computer game on his computer and had not printed out the list. That is most unfortunate for both the prisoners and the public. The very fact that an inmate acknowledges a higher power means he accepts that the world does not revolve around him and his desires. That is very important because the message drummed into their heads by society is "make your own road," "If it feels good do it", and "there are no rules." In actuality, there are rules, and there are consequences for breaking them.

Many studies have found that faith-based programs are effective both in prison and after release. For instance, studies have found that religious offenders exhibit more self-control and are less likely to break the law or commit technical violations, that religious programs serve as a mechanism of self-control that facilitates inmate rehabilitation and reentry, and that religious beliefs are inversely related to a variety of deviant behaviors including alcohol and drug use, and delinquent and criminal activity.

In addition, the American Psychological Association reported[18] that, "among people recovering from substance abuse, a new study finds that higher levels of religious faith and spirituality were associated with several positive mental health outcomes, including more optimism about life and higher resilience to stress, which may help contribute to the recovery process."

One study of the impact of religion on rehabilitation found that religious programs combat the negative effects of prison culture and that religious volunteers are a largely untapped resource pool available to administer educational, vocational, and treatment services at little or no cost.

The National Center on Addiction and Substance Abuse (CASA) at Columbia University released a two-year study[19] that found that "tapping the power of religion and spirituality has enormous potential for lowering the risk of substance abuse among teens and adults and, when combined with professional treatment, for promoting recovery."

In view of these studies, it is important that California prisons offer inmates faith-based options for programs. This means far more than allowing volunteers into prisons to conduct Bible studies. It means offering the option of faith-based drug treatment, life skills, conflict management and education classes.

It has been said that character is what you do when no one is looking. Building the character of prisoners is a vital part of preparing them to be good neighbors.

PAROLE VIOLATIONS MUST HAVE CONSEQUENCES

Too many parole violations have no consequences. Instead, California should mete out swift and certain sanctions for parole violations. But that doesn't mean they have to be sent back to prison since over half of them are "technical violations" – not new crimes. Many offenders don't follow the rules: failing to turn in paperwork, missing an appointment with a parole officer or testing dirty for drugs. But it is very costly – and counter-productive – to send these knuckleheads back to prison.

It would be far more effective, and cost much less, to administer quick, certain and short consequences for breaking the rules. In Hawaii, Judge Stephen Alm, now a district attorney, established Project Hope, which enforces the rules of probation with immediate consequences. If offenders have a dirty urinalysis they are immediately jailed – but not for years, just 24 or 48 hours – enough time to ponder the stupidity of their actions. The object is to get them to follow the rules, without penalizing the taxpayers.

A Pew study[20] found that those offenders who had been in HOPE the longest: 92 percent fewer missed appointments and 96 percent fewer tested positive for drugs. This program accomplishes what we want – teaching offenders to follow the rules and keeping addicts in drug treatment – without filling the prisons.

FOCUS PAROLE OFFICERS ON OFFENDERS WHO POSE THE GREATEST THREAT

California requires every single offender that leaves prison to have a parole agent, regardless of the need or danger to the public. This is a waste of taxpayers' money, and this policy puts Californians in greater danger. I was honored to serve on Gov. Arnold Schwarzenegger's Rehabilitation Strike Team[21] with corrections experts from across the state. Our report stated the problem with this policy clearly: "California's parole system is so over-burdened that parolees who represent a serious public safety risk are not watched closely enough, and those who wish to go straight cannot get the help they need."

A tragic example of the danger of this policy is the sad case of Jaycee Dugard, who was kidnapped[22] when she was 11 years old. Her captor Phillip Garrido had been previously convicted of kidnapping and repeatedly and violently raping a young woman in South Lake Tahoe, the area where little Jaycee was kidnapped when she was 11 years old. Garrido had been released early from his federal sentence and was on supervised parole at the time he kidnapped Jaycee. Parole officers frequently visited his home. Yet, Jaycee went undetected in a tent in his backyard where he imprisoned her.

How did her kidnapper escape detection for so long? Overworked parole officers checked on Garrido many times each year but only peered over the fence at the edge of the property rather than performing a thorough inspection of all the sheds, tents and other enclosures on Garrido's property.

Not one of those officers inquired about the maze of tents and outbuildings or bothered to walk into Garrido's backyard to see what was in them. So, despite this "supervision," Garrido was able to hold young Jaycee as his sex slave – even fathering two children with her - just a few yards from where the parole agents frequently spoke with him on their visits.

The Inspector General's report concluded, "There is little doubt that had they carefully searched the property they would have noticed clothes, diapers or other indications that several females were living back there. That should have sent off alarms immediately."[23]

Parole officers should be paying much closer attention to high-risk offenders rather than giving the same attention to check kiters. It's not rocket science.

As Michael Alpert, Chair of the Little Hoover Commission said, "These laws have not been tough on crime, but they have been tough on taxpayers."

MAKE PRISONS SAFER FOR STAFF, VOLUNTEERS AND INMATES

Prisoners should be protected from assaults inside prison. No crime, no matter how heinous, includes being beaten and raped as part of the sentence. Since the government prevents inmates from defending themselves, it is incumbent on the government to protect them. Prison officials that tolerate violent prisons encourage "soft" inmates to become street gladiators to survive. That's not good for the staff, volunteers, inmates and particularly for our communities.

One horrible example is Rodney Hulin,[24] a young, slight, handsome inmate who was imprisoned in Texas for lighting a trash dumpster on fire as a prank. That turned a prank into a tragedy because arson is classified as a violent felony. Rodney was sent to "the big house." From the day he arrived, he was beaten and raped daily. In desperation, Rodney went to the corrections supervisor to ask for help. The officer told him, "You got a choice. Fight or f*ck". Rodney decided he could not take any more of this abuse, so he killed himself.

While prisoner rape is often the source of jokes on late night TV, Rodney is proof that it is all too real. The Bureau of Justice Statistics found that at least 10 percent of inmates are sexually assaulted every year.[25] And heartbreakingly, corrections staff are responsible for 42 percent of those assaults.

SENTENCES SHOULD MATCH THE SEVERITY OF THE CRIME

Rodney's case highlights another flaw in our system: one-size-fits-all sentences. Cases should be decided individually, not as an assembly line. The harm done by a sentence should never be greater than the harm caused by the crime.

VOLUNTEERS OFFER SOMETHING GOVERNMENT CANNOT

Dr. Martin Luther King, Jr. said, "To change someone you must first love them, and they must know that they are loved." Government programs can't love prisoners, but volunteers can. Prisons should make a priority of matching inmates with mentors, responsible members of the community, who can help inmates prepare a life plan to stay out of trouble when they return to the community. The mentors will walk with them as they take the first difficult steps in freedom, helping them find a job and avoid temptations.

Having a good, moral person to help offenders think through the decisions that confront them as they leave prison makes a huge difference in whether they can stay out of trouble and become contributing members of the community. Yet, California prohibits mentors who have worked with prisoners inside prison from staying in touch with them after they are released. This prevents inmates from having access to the very people that can help them succeed. No wonder our recidivism rate is so high. It's time to stop turning away the helping hands of mentors.

Moving Forward

California needs to get crime under control. Too many people are being victimized every day due to the malfeasance of the government. Californians deserve better. These reforms have been implemented in other states, and their people are safer, and they have lower recidivism. Now, Californians must demand that their state and local governments adopt them.

Pat Nolan is the director of the American Conservative Union Foundation's Center for Criminal Justice Reform and a former California Assembly member.

CHAPTER EIGHT: BUILDING A SUSTAINABLE BUDGET

CHAPTER EIGHT
BUILDING A SUSTAINABLE BUDGET

By Richard Mersereau

*Facts are stubborn things; and whatever may be our wishes,
our inclinations, or the dictates of our passion, they cannot
alter the state of facts and evidence.*
— John Adams

Our state and nation have recently emerged from the unprecedented year-long "COVID quarantine." The pandemic's impact on virtually every aspect of the lives of nearly 40 million Californians and its profound human toll are incalculable, and properly remain foremost in our minds.

Long before the emergence of the coronavirus, however, successive gubernatorial administrations and the California Legislature abdicated their responsibilities: Even as total and per capita state government revenues grew significantly in real, inflation-adjusted terms, the state's long-term debt obligations and baseline budget spending grew by far more. The cumulative result is a looming fiscal crisis of unprecedented size and scope. It will impede California's economic growth and diminish the quality of life of most Californians long after the economic dislocations of the state's COVID response fade from memory, proving particularly devastating for those at the bottom of the economic ladder who rely on government most.

In his 2020 State of the State address, given mere weeks before the state and nation were plunged into crisis, Gov. Gavin Newsom noted that California was "enjoying 118 consecutive months of net job growth, (with) some 3.4 million jobs created since the Great Recession... We've built a record reserve, including the largest rainy-day fund in state history. We've achieved the highest credit rating in nearly two decades. And we've disappeared the infamous wall of debt..."

Which view of California's economy and fiscal condition is true? Both are. Herein lies the problem.

Since the end of the Great Recession, the state general fund has not merely recovered, but has grown significantly. Since the 2013-14 budget year, per capita expenditures have grown roughly 53 percent in nominal terms, and nearly a third in inflation-adjusted terms:[1]

FIGURE 1
Schedule 6 at 2021-22 Governor's Budget
Summary of State Population, Employees, and Expenditures

					Revenue		Expenditures		Expenditures per Capita		Expenditures per $100 of Personal Income	
Year	Population[1]/ (Thousands)	Employees[2]/	Employees per 1,000 Population	Personal Income[3]/ (Billions)	General Fund (Millions)	Total (Millions)	General Fund[4]/ (Millions)	Total[5]/ (Millions)	General Fund[4]/	Total[5]/	General Fund[4]/	Total[5]/
2005-06	35,986	317,593	8.8	1,396.2	93,427	118,331	91,592	119,612	2,545.21	3,323.85	6.56	8.57
2006-07	36,247	335,384	9.3	1,499.5	95,415	120,663	101,413	129,968	2,797.83	3,585.62	6.76	8.67
2007-08	36,553	343,118	9.4	1,564.4	102,574	127,194	102,986	138,065	2,817.44	3,777.12	6.58	8.83
2008-09	36,856	350,609	9.5	1,596.3	82,772	106,319	90,940	122,386	2,467.44	3,320.65	5.70	7.67
2009-10	37,077	345,777	9.3	1,536.4	87,041	109,989	87,237	117,001	2,352.86	3,155.62	5.68	7.62
2010-11	37,339	371,959	10.0	1,579.1	93,489	122,463	91,549	130,981	2,451.83	3,507.89	5.80	8.29
2011-12	37,676	356,808	9.5	1,683.2	87,071	118,792	86,404	126,361	2,293.34	3,353.89	5.13	7.51
2012-13	38,038	346,321	9.1	1,805.2	99,915	137,242	96,562	141,001	2,538.57	3,706.85	5.35	7.81
2013-14	38,370	353,979	9.2	1,856.6	102,675	142,860	99,838	142,810	2,601.98	3,721.92	5.38	7.69
2014-15	38,729	360,859	9.3	1,939.5	111,318	157,875	112,974	160,294	2,917.04	4,138.86	5.82	8.26
2015-16	39,060	350,680	9.0	2,103.7	115,500	161,759	113,984	160,209	2,918.18	4,101.61	5.42	7.62
2016-17	39,321	361,743	9.2	2,212.7	119,982	167,036	119,291	165,880	3,033.77	4,218.61	5.39	7.50
2017-18	39,612	368,520	9.3	2,364.1	131,116	188,115	124,756	177,316	3,149.45	4,476.32	5.28	7.50
2018-19	39,672	376,990	9.5	2,514.1	140,060	201,754	140,387	203,243	3,538.69	5,123.08	5.58	8.08
2019-20	39,761	382,465	9.6	2,632.3	140,623	200,496	146,556	208,272	3,685.92	5,238.10	5.57	7.91
2020-21	39,782	390,735	9.8	2,761.8	162,742	214,897	155,898	226,950	3,918.81	5,704.84	5.64	8.22
2021-22	39,964	388,591	9.7	2,635.2	158,370	219,534	164,516	227,238	4,116.60	5,686.07	6.24	8.62

Source: 2021-22 Governor's Budget Summary

So how could California's fiscal condition be anything but rosy? While California's General Fund revenues increased significantly as the economy recovered, state government spending grew greater still.[2]

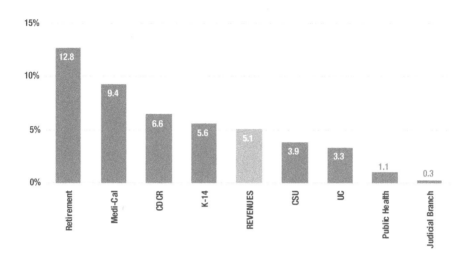

Source: David Crane, Stanford Institute for Economic Policy Research

According to a November 2020 report by the nonpartisan Legislative Analyst's Office (LAO), "general fund revenues from the state's three largest sources would grow at an average annual rate of less than 1 percent. Meanwhile, general fund expenditures under current law and policy grow at an average 4.4 percent per year. The net result is that the state faces an operating deficit, which is relatively small in 2021-22, but grows to around $17 billion by 2024-25."[3] The Governor's Budget, while more optimistic (1.9 percent growth rate through 2024-2025), warns this figure "...is far lower than the average growth rate since the 2009-10 fiscal year of 6.4 percent."[4] This calculation does not include *any* of the unprecedented federal revenues from successive "COVID relief bills" or the record realization of capital gains tax proceeds.

In just three years, the operating deficit for the state's "current baseline budget" will equal all general fund support for the 23-campus California State University system – times four.[5] The phrase "current baseline budget" is key: it assumes no additional spending, no new programs, and all other actuarial and caseload assumptions remaining unchanged. That simply does not represent reality.

California's general fund derives from three principal sources: Personal Income Tax (PIT), the Corporation Tax, and the state sales and use tax (local government add-ons increase the rate paid in each county and city). Each of these "Big Three" taxes are among the highest in the nation.

Currently, the top 1 percent of California taxpayers pay roughly 46 percent of all personal income taxes. The top 5 percent of taxpayers account for more than 67 percent of all PIT revenues.[6] The spike in PIT revenues resulting from California taxing capital gains realizations at the highest marginal rate (as high as 13.3 percent, while at this writing the combined federal capital gains tax rate is 23.8 percent) is by its nature limited.

FIGURE 3
Capital Gains Realizations
(Dollars in Billions)

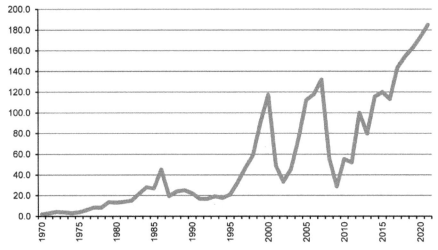

Source: 2021-22 Governor's Budget Summary

Some would argue the current full funding of the Budget Stabilization Account – together with two optional deposits above the constitutionally required minimum in recent years, and the direct "paying down" of pension debt in successive budgets – are indicative of the state's strong fiscal position.[7] In fact, it demonstrates the opposite. However laudable these efforts (and they are), they were undertaken during a period of solid growth in both the economy and tax revenues. Capital gains revenues have grown sixfold since 2009, and more than 250 percent as a percentage of general fund revenues. The precipitous decline in revenues from 2007-2008 to 2013-14 are instructive.[8]

For decades, criticism has been leveled against California's Corporation Tax by those who believe it should be significantly increased. The push for more taxes is relentless. Consider recent efforts to impose a split roll property tax on California businesses and the three-year, $9.2-billion tax increase imposed by Assembly Bill 85 (2020), which suspended numerous tax credits and deductions for business losses, research and development for the 2020, 2021 and 2022 tax years. The reasons for the exodus of companies from California is evident.

Unlike 40 to 50 years ago, today California (and U.S.) businesses face far greater competition from overseas competitors. According to the Organization for Economic Co-operation and Development (OECD), even after passage of the 2017 Tax Cut and Jobs Act (TCJA), which reduced the top federal corporate income tax rate from 35 percent to 21 percent, U.S. corporations face an effective average tax rate of 24.6 percent in 2019, not including the California Corporation Tax of 8.84 percent. This ranks above the non-U.S. average of 21.9 percent, is 13th highest out of 37 countries in the OECD and is higher than the tax rate imposed by the People's Republic of China. Prior to enactment of the TCJA, the U.S. effective average tax rate for corporate investment was the highest in the OECD at 37.5 percent, again not including the California Corporation Tax.[9]

The last of California's Big Three state tax revenue sources (property tax being overwhelmingly a source of local government funds) – the state sales tax – merits far greater discussion than space allows. For purpose of this chapter, however, the incidence of California's combined state and local sales tax ranks among the highest in the nation, and in many instances exceeds the total sales tax levy of several states that impose no income tax at all.

Sales taxes are among the most regressive of taxes despite numerous (and appropriate) exemptions for food, medicine and other essentials. Given California policymakers' stated concern for the poor, why has every effort at tax "reform" in the last decade sought to expand the sales tax to services, and in almost every instance has done so in a manner that would disproportionately affect lower- and middle-class Californians? The answer is as plain as why Willie Sutton robbed banks: Because that's where the money is. As Sen. Robert Hertzberg told the *Los Angeles Times* upon introduction of his Senate Bill 8 of 2015, "To me, if you can't raise $10 billion (a year) it's not worth the effort."[10]

Twenty years ago, California state government – and local governments as well – staked much of our fiscal future on the promise of an ever-growing stock market. Senate Bill 400 of 1999, which enacted major retroactive increases in the pension benefits of most state workers, was explicitly represented to the Legislature by the California Public Employees' Retirement System (CalPERS) as having no cost to the state General Fund for its first 10 years by relying solely on changes in accounting and investment returns.[11]

SB 400 has proven devastating for state and local government budgets. A public employee pension plan that once was fully funded now has an unfunded liability of more than $167 billion by conservative estimates. Despite modest reforms and increased payments by the state, the total pension liability has grown by more than $100 billion in the last 10 years.

FIGURE 4
Funding Progress – Unfunded Liability and Funded Ratios

Actuarial Valuation Date	Actuarial Value of Assets	Actuarial Accrued Liability (AAL) (Entry Age)	Unfunded AAL (UAAL)/ Surplus (AVA Basis)	Funded Ratio (Actuarial Value of Assets Basis)	Annual Covered Payroll	UAAL/ Surplus as a % of Covered Payroll	Market Value of Assets (MVA)	Unfunded AAL (UAAL)/ Surplus (MVA Basis)	Funded Ratio (Market Value of Assets Basis)
	(1)	(2)	(3) = (2) - (1)	(4) = (1) / (2)	(5)	(6) = (3) / (5)	(7)	(8) = (2) - (7)	(9) = (7) / (2)
PERF (Dollars in Millions)									
06/30/19	$372,778	$531,166	$158,388	70.2%	$56,391	280.9%	$372,778	$158,388	70.2%
06/30/18	354,616	504,996	150,380	70.2%	53,903	279.0%	354,616	150,380	70.2%
06/30/17	326,182	465,046	138,864	70.1%	51,991	267.1%	326,182	138,864	70.1%
06/30/16	298,126	436,703	138,577	68.3%	49,833	278.1%	298,126	138,577	68.3%
06/30/15	302,418	413,700	111,282	73.1%	47,458	234.5%	302,418	111,282	73.1%
06/30/14	301,257	394,726	93,469	76.3%	44,958	207.9%	301,257	93,469	76.3%
06/30/13	281,928	375,019	93,091	75.2%	42,575	218.7%	261,622	113,397	69.8%
06/30/12	282,991	340,429	57,438	83.1%	42,599	134.8%	236,800	103,629	69.6%
06/30/11	271,389	328,567	57,178	82.6%	43,901	130.2%	241,740	86,827	73.6%
06/30/10	257,070	308,343	51,273	83.4%	44,984	114.0%	201,632	106,711	65.4%

Source: 2021-22 Governor's Budget Summary

If the discount rate (estimated annual return) is just one point lower than the fund's estimate of 7 percent, the increased unfunded liability for just one group of retirees (state miscellaneous employees) grows by more than $14 billion, and nearly $7 billion for state peace officers and firefighters.[12] In 2019-20, CalPERS posted a 4.7-percent return. Over the last 20 years, the average annual return is 5.5 percent.[13]

The same is true with respect to OPEB – Other Post-Employment Benefits – for retired public employees. If the "blended discount rate" for OPEB benefits for just the nine bargaining units of state employees represented by the Service Employees International Union is off by 1 percent, the increase in net OPEB liability is nearly $6 billion.[14] Similarly, if the estimated health-care-cost trend rate for these same nine bargaining units is only 1 percent higher than estimated, that adds an additional $6 billion in liability.[15]

The conduct – and unsurprisingly, the fiscal positions – of our state's teachers' and university pension systems have been equally dismal. After a 20-year pension holiday, when employees did not make a single contribution to their own retirement, the University of California was forced to borrow $2.7 billion to shore up its pension program. With normal contributions, no borrowing would have been necessary.[16] Similarly, according to the independent auditor's report of the California State Teachers' Retirement System for the fiscal year ending June 30, 2020, "the value of the State Teachers' Retirement Plan (STRP) total pension liability exceeded the STRP fiduciary net position by $96.9 billion."[17]

As UCLA economist and Hoover Institution scholar Lee Ohanian emphasizes in his December 2020 UC Berkeley Baxter Lecture, the policy and governance missteps that are the primary reasons for the state's once and future crises are deeply rooted in a lack of proper incentives and a lack of accountability within our government institutions.[18] The monumental failures of the Employment Development Department, the Department of Motor Vehicles, Fi$Cal (the state's budgeting and IT system), and the High Speed Rail boondoggle are merely the highest profile examples of a systemic failure of governance.

Despite record levels of spending and debt, Californians face the highest rates of homelessness, income inequality and welfare dependency in the nation. These never-ending promises and ideological excesses instead brought about the highest gasoline and electricity costs in the nation, sky-rocketing home costs, and some of the highest taxes in the nation, all while reducing essential government services and incurring staggering levels of debt. In the words of Winston Churchill, "However beautiful the strategy, one should occasionally look at the results."

Notwithstanding this sad legacy of imprudence and mismanagement, California can change its trajectory and enact meaningful reforms that place California's government on a solid, sustainable financial footing. Here are some brief recommendations:

First, Do No Economic Harm

By executive order but particularly through legislation, every year California places ever-greater burdens upon the private sector. There is simply no way – and quite frankly, no will in either party, in particular the dominant Democratic super-majority – to "squeeze, cut and trim" the California budget to address this coming budget crisis. There is also no way that government – state or federal – can or will provide on an indefinite basis the majority of income support, childcare, healthcare and housing for a significant and growing percentage of California's population. The only answer is sustained economic growth, providing more after-tax income for working Californians and sufficient tax revenues for essential services. The first answer is temperamental: California lawmakers need to appreciate the importance of its still-vibrant private sector and stop imposing costly new burdens upon it.

A New Vision for California Government

California government employs roughly the same number of employees as a percentage of the state's population as it did before the introduction of the personal computer. In 2015 and again in 2018, the state auditor detailed the "graying" of California's state workforce and called for all agencies to undertake succession planning.[19] By developing – and making available online – explicit performance and productivity enhancements and metrics across California state government, even a 1-3 percent cost reduction will make a real difference. Current failures such as the disgraceful EDD fraud case, 30 percent DMV absentee rates, and multibillion-dollar cost overruns at FI$Cal must be fully examined, disclosed to the public, and practices put in place to ensure such failures never happen again. Just one change long advocated by the LAO – the elimination of as many as 3,500 unnecessary Caltrans positions – has been estimated to save up to $500 million a year.[20]

Across the nation, states of all sizes offer examples of success in areas where California government falls short. Other states spend far less on road construction and repair, prisons and other "deliverables," while creating an environment where construction costs, permitting, regulatory fees, threats of litigation costs, workers compensation and other expenses are far less burdensome. Implementing "best practices" from other states, as well as from our own local governments, can result in significant cost savings in all areas of government. For example, if EDD had listened to and implemented the recommendations of local district attorneys respecting welfare fraud prior to COVID, the result would be literally billions of dollars of taxpayer savings.

In the "post-COVID moment," the governor and Legislature should undertake a comprehensive review of all regulations affecting private businesses and professions, as well as taxpayer-funded services like tele-medicine (including across state lines). They should examine if rules suspended during the shutdown can be eliminated on a permanent basis. California's current "sunset review" process is woefully inadequate and should actually begin to eliminate unnecessary regulations and bureaucracy. Occupational licensing reforms will particularly enhance the economic prospects of lower-income workers.

When Governor Schwarzenegger took office, he promised to "blow up the boxes" and reform an inefficient, ineffective state government by means of his "California Performance Review." While this effort failed in large part due to partisan opposition, institutional inertia and hubris, Article V, Section 6 of the California Constitution provides the governor with the authority to "assign and reorganize functions among executive officers and agencies and their employees." A Governor's Reorganization Plan (GRP) is a rarely used process by which agency and department consolidation, streamlining and, as the name suggests, reorganization can occur. Rather than undertake a wholesale effort to restructure California government, a GRP to consolidate all state housing entities under a single, accountable entity could provide an important first step and "proof of concept" for additional reform. The newly-created entity would align authority with accountability, eliminate unnecessary and redundant costs, provide a single point of contact for the private sector, and allow the public to focus their attention directly on that part of government responsible for either the success or failure of the task.

Lawmakers Must Play by the Rules

Both houses of the Legislature must ensure that every bill will receive a full and fair hearing upon the request of the author. The current Assembly practice (enabled by a change in rules) allowing a committee chair to unilaterally refuse to hear a bill is an affront to every Californian, and ensures that neither reform, oversight nor accountability can occur. As two Assembly members – one Democrat, one Republican – have written, "There are numerous examples of (other) bills that have been denied hearings for various reasons–more often than not, based on politics. The public deserves to have their voices and legislative ideas heard. For the sake of our constituents and all Californians, we should not be censoring what comes before the Legislature. This path is sure to lead us down a dark road that is anything but democratic."[21]

Similarly, the Assembly must adhere to the letter and spirit of Proposition 54 of 2016, which requires all bills to be in print and available online for 72 hours before a vote. The Assembly has acted in clear contravention of the Constitution in denying the people the ability to review a bill and engage their elected officials prior to a vote "in the house of origin." Such tortured interpretations limit public notice and debate, and thwart any semblance of open, accountable and transparent government.

The Legislature should end the practice – and the governor should not sign – any bill in which the Legislature includes a "de minimis" $1,000 appropriation in a "budget-related bill" to allow a controversial piece of unrelated policy legislation to be passed by simple majority vote, take immediate effect, and not be subject to referendum. This cynical manipulation of Proposition 25 of 2010 to frustrate the will of the people must end.

Some Other Modest Proposals

As the current Legislature and governor will not act, the people need to invoke their reserve right of initiative to draft, qualify and pass a carefully crafted constitutional amendment to address the state's pension crisis. Despite two recent state Supreme Court rulings upholding minor changes to public employee retirement plans addressing pension spiking and "air time," the "California rule" that prohibits changes on a forward-going basis to current government employees remains in effect. Under the California rule, a court must "determine whether the modification imposes disadvantages on affected employees." It must then determine "whether the disadvantages are accompanied by comparable new advantages." If not, the court must decide "whether the (legislative body's) purpose in making the changes was sufficient, for constitutional purposes, to justify an impairment of pension rights." And if so, we need to decide whether it's acceptable, in light of these legitimate purposes, to proceed without providing comparable advantages to the affected employees."[22]

No other state interprets its public employee pension laws in this manner. Democrat former governor of Rhode Island and current U.S. Secretary of Commerce Gina Raimondo could not have addressed that state's pension crisis if the "California rule" were applied in her state.[23] Not only is the fiscal stability of California state and local government at risk, but the pensions of all current and future retirees are in danger of being significantly impaired – and ultimately reduced – if the "California rule" is not addressed soon.

California once again must dedicate general fund revenues each year to pay for vital public works projects. During the Pat Brown and Ronald Reagan eras, a significant percentage of long-term infrastructure projects were financed with general fund revenues. One potential model, Assembly Constitutional Amendment 27 of 2006, authored by then-Assembly Minority Leader (and now U.S. House Minority Leader) Kevin McCarthy, began with as little as 1 percent or $750 million, with funds growing over time to provide significant revenues for vital infrastructure projects without raising taxes.[24] This approach would help prioritize fundamental infrastructure spending while imposing necessary fiscal discipline.

On this point, California should end the continued waste of the High-Speed Rail (HSR) project, dedicating all remaining funds to "jump start" far more vital infrastructure projects. Sold to the voters in 2008 as a project requiring no additional taxpayer funds for construction or operation, cruising at 200-plus miles an hour from San Francisco to Los Angeles – and ultimately to San Diego – by the year 2020, and completed for around $33 billion[25], HSR has failed every test, and will cost more than triple the initial amount while no longer even pretending to serve San Diego. An ever-growing chorus of legislators, Democrat and Republican, are willing to acknowledge reality and re-direct billions of tax dollars – including $4.1 billion in unappropriated HSR bond funds, together with 25 percent of all greenhouse gas revenues continuously appropriated to HSR – to far better use.

For decades, California's constitutional spending cap – the "Gann Limit" – has largely been a dead letter, providing no meaningful limit on state spending as even California's sky-high tax rates weren't sufficient to trigger the spending ceiling. Even then, the LAO was critical of efforts by then-Gov. Jerry Brown to find ways to evade the Gann Limit[26]. However, the LAO recently determined that because state tax revenues have grown so high in 2021, the Gann Limit might require refunds to taxpayers in future years.[27]

While the voters and taxpayers of Colorado in November 2019 were able to retain their "TABOR" (Taxpayer Bill of Rights), with the passage of the 2021-22 California state budget Governor Newsom and the California Legislature actively sought to spend all available revenues and prevent across-the-board taxpayer rebates and rate reductions, while cynically manipulating the Gann Limit to allow for even greater spending. If we are ever to have a chance in restoring our state's fiscal condition, California taxpayers must stand firm in limiting annual increases in state government spending to no greater than the sum of population and inflation."

Since 1978, Proposition 13 has stood as a bulwark against higher taxes. Recently, however, state Supreme Court decisions and repeated efforts to amend Prop 13 to provide a "split roll" allowing higher taxes on commercial property threaten this landmark measure. While it is essential to "hold the line" on higher taxes to protect working families and ensure an environment where innovation and job creation can flourish, thoughtful, equitable efforts to grow tax proceeds to fund vital government services exist that do not result in higher taxes.

One Parting 'Moonshot'

Texas and Florida – the second and third most populous states – are proof positive that "part-time" legislatures need not be consigned to our smallest, least populated states. Far more than a mere "thought experiment," the prospect of California fundamentally altering its state government to introduce and pass all but emergency legislation in even-numbered years, while enacting a two-year budget and focusing solely on government oversight and reform with no bill introductions in odd-numbered years offers a unique opportunity to right the California ship of state. While legal experts might dispute whether such a reform must first be proposed by the Legislature as opposed to the people consistent with Article XVIII of the California Constitution's prohibition of a "constitutional revision," the prospect of reducing the flood of dilatory (and destructive) bill introductions while focusing our elected officials' attention on improving and reforming government has genuine merit.

Richard Mersereau is the former chief consultant to the California State Assembly Committee on Revenue and Taxation and the Senate Committee on Constitutional Amendments. He served as director of the Assembly Republican Caucus Office of Policy under 10 elected Assembly Republican Leaders, as well as president of the Sacramento County Taxpayers League, a member of the Taxation Committee of the California Chamber of Commerce, and as a visiting scholar at the Cal Poly Institute for Advanced Technology and Public Policy.

**CHAPTER NINE: CALIFORNIA BURNING—
WILDFIRES AND CLIMATE CHANGE**

CHAPTER NINE
CALIFORNIA BURNING:
WILDFIRES AND CLIMATE CHANGE

By Daniel M. Kolkey

"The dogmas of the quiet past are inadequate to the stormy present."

— *Abraham Lincoln*

Californians in 2020 experienced five of the state's six largest wildfires in at least a century due mainly to the effects of drought. They also suffered two nights of rolling power outages during an unexpectedly severe heat wave. These tribulations followed 2019's power outages that lasted days when high winds compelled utilities to shut down to avoid downed power lines from triggering wildfires.

Instead of focusing on new strategies to help control the state's wildfire risk, Gov. Gavin Newsom announced in September 2020, that California needed to get more "aggressive" in achieving its target of 100 percent green electricity, stating that the state's target date of 2045 is "too late." He asserted that the state needs to "fast track all of these efforts," including investing in green energy and "getting more electric cars on the road."

Yet, California only accounts for roughly 1 percent of global emissions; thus, there is no guarantee that the state's ambitious climate change policy is going to have any effect on arresting climate change, let alone reduce the risk of wildfires. Instead, the state should prioritize policies that mitigate the consequences of climate change over the hope of arresting climate change.

None of this means, of course, that California should cease its efforts to encourage the generation of renewable energy. But it does mean that California must engage in a more rational policy that balances additional reductions in greenhouse gases against the cost of those reductions and the diversion of resources that could have gone to addressing the consequences of climate change, like more devastating wildfires.

Unfortunately, the state has focused more on arbitrary goals for reducing greenhouse gases tomorrow than protecting Californians today. Within five years of California's enactment of the Global Warming Solutions Act of 2006 to reduce its greenhouse gases to 1990 levels by 2020, the Legislature escalated its green energy mandates. In 2011, the Legislature passed a statute to require retail sellers of electricity to derive at least 33 percent of retail sales from renewable energy by Dec. 31, 2020.[1] Five years later, it required retail sellers to derive 50 percent of electricity from renewable sources by Dec. 31, 2030.[2] In 2018, it escalated its green energy goals to require the state to derive 60 percent of electricity from renewable energy resources by 2030.[3] It also set a new goal of achieving 100 percent of electricity from renewable or zero-carbon sources by 2045.

The state should have instead weighed the marginal benefit of further accelerating its green energy goals against the increased cost of energy to the public and the diversion of resources away from measures necessary to mitigate the consequences of climate change, including the increasing wildfire risk. These measures must include thinning unhealthy forests susceptible to raging fires and strengthening California's aging energy infrastructure, which has increased the risk of power outages and wildfires during high winds that down power lines. Indeed, the nonpartisan California Legislative Analyst's Office (LAO) reports that "[u]tility power lines caused at least 8 of the 20 most destructive fires (40 percent) in California's history," with six occurring since 2015.[4]

This chapter proposes policies that will help California protect against its wildfire risks without undermining its climate goals.

Wildfires: The Challenges

Droughts are not a new experience for California. Even when California became a state in 1850, it was suffering from a drought that lasted until 1861.[5] More than 87 years ago, it suffered one of its longest droughts, which lasted seven years from 1928-1934.

But recent climate changes have increased the threat of drought and wildfires. As the LAO observes, "Climate scientists project that climate change will contribute to hotter weather and longer dry seasons in California than was previously typical," which, in turn, "negatively affect forest health and increase wildfire risks."[6] According to Daniel Swain, a scientist at UCLA, this warming results in extra evaporation from the soil, resulting in drier vegetation.[7] And warmer waters have pushed some tropical storms north in the Pacific, which led to 15,000 lightning strikes in August 2020, which, in turn, sparked hundreds of wildfires in California, according to Wally Covington, an emeritus professor of forestry at Northern Arizona University.[8]

There is no question that the three droughts since 2000 have been particularly deadly for California wildfires. Dead timber, dry brush, and kindling, awaiting fires' fury, built up for the perfect firestorms.

Thus, in 2017, Californians suffered the seventh largest fire (the Thomas Fire) since reliable record keeping in 1932, plus the Nuns Fire, the Atlas Fire and the Tubbs Fire, which crossed a six-lane freeway into northern Santa Rosa to become one of the state's most destructive wildfires in terms of buildings burned.

The next year saw the 2018 Mendocino Complex Fire, which burned 459,123 acres – the only wildfire to eclipse 300,000 acres since the start of reliable record-keeping – plus the Carr Fire (burning 229,651 acres), the Camp Fire (destroying the town of Paradise) and the Woolsey Fire (burning 1,643 structures).

But 2020 witnessed five of the 10 largest wildfires in California in modern times. While multiple fires earlier that year were contained reasonably promptly, in mid-August two tropical storms generated nearly 15,000 lightning strikes onto forests and brush in Northern California, triggering hundreds of fires.[9] Additional fires, fueled by high winds, were triggered in September following record-setting temperatures in the north and south.[10] The August Complex Fire alone burned 846,732 acres; the SCU Complex and LNU Complex fires burned more than 300,000 acres each; and the North Complex Fire destroyed nearly 300,000 acres. Dense smoke filled the air for weeks and damaged Californians' health, even where the fires spared their homes and businesses.

Ironically, these wildfires undermined California's climate-change policies. Devastating fires not only reduce the role that California's forests play as a "sink" to sequester carbon emissions from the atmosphere, but they also neutralize the benefits of the state's carbon emission reductions. For instance, the fires in 2018 released more than 45 million metric tons of carbon dioxide into the atmosphere, producing more than nine times more emissions than were reduced in 2017, according to a report by Beacon Economics for the Next 10 think tank.[11] These fires also undermine air quality. One study, cited by the LAO, estimates that "wildfires account for up to 25 percent of small particulate matter air pollution in the U.S. in recent years."[12]

Because California's government cannot rely on its climate-change goals to control California's increased wildfire risk, it must implement and fund new policies to expedite the thinning of forests and the removal of dead timber and brush from its millions of acres of forests. This can be done through new techniques, new legislative initiatives, and if necessary, the governor's emergency powers. The state must encourage fire resistance measures near wildland-urban interfaces and strengthen the state's aging energy grid, which has sparked wildfires.

Better Utilizing the Greenhouse Gas Reduction Fund

As an initial matter, more and sustained funding will be necessary to support efforts to thin millions of acres of forests and remove dead timber and dry brush upon which fires prey at an alarmingly rapid rate. Len Nielson, the staff chief for prescribed fire and environmental protection at the California Department of Forestry and Fire Protection (known as CAL FIRE), acknowledged that the agency has more than 500 planned burns and other fuel-reduction projects, but is awaiting funding, resources and personnel.[13]

Fortunately, there is an existing fund that should be dedicated to addressing the consequences of climate change: California's Greenhouse Gas Reduction Fund, which is funded by the sale of carbon credits as part of California's climate-change policy.

Yet, according to the LAO, 68 percent of the funds in Greenhouse Gas Reduction Fund during the 2020-2021 budget cycle went to a grab bag of projects other than addressing the consequences of climate change.[14] For instance, the state allocated $499 million to the High Speed Rail Authority, $399 million to "affordable housing and sustainable communities," $200 million to "transit and intercity rail capital," another $100 million to "transit operations," and only $200 million to "healthy and resilient forests," which would include prescribed burns to thin forests.[15]

Given the urgent need for more and sustained resources to address the consequences of climate change, the state should re-allocate funds from high-speed rail and transit-related projects to wildfire mitigation efforts and to the strengthening of California's energy infrastructure, which has sparked six of the most destructive fires since 2015. After all, what is more urgent – funding for *tomorrow's* high-speed rail, or saving *today's* lives and homes from wildfires (which, by the way, may generate more carbon than the transit projects save)?

Thinning Unhealthy Forests

Decades of fire suppression have resulted in dense forests that include small trees, dead timber and brush, which in arid climates can serve as "ladder fuels" that carry flames to the trees' canopies and spread.[16] Ironically, Native Americans used controlled burns in forests to reduce such wildfire risks, but, until recently, the state has rejected such ancient wisdom in favor of rapidly putting out fires.

Many experts now argue that prescribed burns can reduce the buildup of dead or diseased trees, dry grass, and withered shrubs that serve as ignition switches for wildfires.[17] According to acclaimed nature and science author, Gary Ferguson, thinning forests reduce fire intensity by reducing the number of young, tightly spaced trees, which are flammable.[18] Thinning also reduces competition among trees for water, keeping the remaining trees healthier and "thus more resistant to insects and disease"; and by reducing the forest's canopy, thinning allows more rain to reach the ground.[19] Moreover, one scholarly study suggests that thinning can also reduce pine beetle infestations that kill trees that serve as fuel for fire.[20]

Controlled burns can be effective. Prescribed burns slowed the advance of the California Rim Fire in 2013 to permit firefighters to get ahead of the burn, saving a number of homes.[21] Likewise, in 2019, CAL FIRE engaged in thinning and controlled burns, which helped contain the Creek Fire in 2020.[22] In 2021, the California Governor's Office acknowledged that "[p]rescribed fire ...is now well-recognized as one of the most versatile and cost-effective tools available to reduce fuels buildup in forests and the risk of catastrophic wildfires."[23]

Yet, despite the benefits of forest thinning, the U.S. Forest Service only oversaw controlled burns of 44,000 acres in California in 2020, and the total amount of land subject to controlled burns in California averaged only 125,000 acres a year – a small fraction of the 15 million acres of California forest in need of restoration.[24]

Thinning California's forests will not be easy. California has 33 million acres of forest.[25] According to a joint report prepared by CAL FIRE and other state agencies, "more than 129 million trees, primarily in the Sierra Nevada, have died from drought and insects since 2010,"[26] and roughly 15 million acres of California's forests need some form of treatment.[27] Those 15 million acres are "composed of approximately 10 million acres of federal lands and 5 million acres of private and other public lands ranked as high priority for reducing wildfire threats to maintain ecological health."[28] State and local governments only own 1 million acres.[29]

However, the privately owned forest lands, which constitute roughly 12.5 million acres of California's forest lands (roughly 38 percent of California's total), are considered a public trust resource that is subject to state regulation.[30] Accordingly, with nearly 40 percent of forest lands subject to state regulation, there is much the state can do.

Yet, the state's progress has been slow and its vision wanting. In late 2019, the state certified an environmental impact review of a "California Vegetation Treatment Program" that will facilitate the removal of vegetation to retard the spread of wildfires to structures and create fuel breaks. However, its objective is to cover only 250,000 acres annually on non-federal lands.[31] Moreover, CAL FIRE is merely accepting applications from local governments to take advantage of the program.

There is merit in receiving applications from local governments regarding areas in need of fire suppression since local governments are presumably most familiar with their local conditions. However, of the $536 million in additional funding for wildfire prevention and resiliency that the governor announced in April 2021 as part of the state's 2020-2021 budget, only $155 million will be going to CAL FIRE's grants.[32] More significantly, there is no overall strategy for addressing the wildfire risk (although the governor's office has suggested that one is coming "by the spring of 2021"[33]). Despite an unexpected windfall of tax revenues in 2021, the governor's May Revision for the 2021-2022 budget proposes only $100 million more for such CAL FIRE grants.[34]

Other recent initiatives have also been too modest to rise to the challenge. In August 2020, Gavin Newsom and the U.S. Forest Service announced a joint effort to use controlled burns and debris removal on 1 million acres of California forests annually to reduce wildfire risks. But in January 2021 the governor's office suggested that CAL FIRE would "use all fuels reduction methods, including prescribed fire, to expand its fuel reduction program with a goal of treating [only] 100,000 acres of its 500,000-acre target," which it would seek to reach "by 2025."[35] By comparison, Florida's forest service authorizes 2.1 million acres of controlled fires annually, according to the Florida agriculture department.

In May 2021, the governor's office submitted its May Revise for the state's 2021-2022 budget, which proposes a total of $608 million for "resilient forests & landscapes" (including the $100 million in CAL FIRE grants) and "wildfire fuel breaks."[36] But it still has no overall strategy for thinning forests, and the *$608 million* in proposed appropriations pales in comparison with the *$2.575 billion* proposed for "climate resistance ($784 million) and "zero emission vehicle acceleration ($1.8 billion).[37] In short, the funding does not rise to the urgent challenge of protecting lives, livelihoods and homes.

Legislation to Streamline Prescribed Burns

Even with adequate funding, California imposes many legal hurdles that delay and thwart effective action for thinning forests. Consider the following:

> The California Environmental Quality Act (CEQA) and Z'berg Nejedly Forest Practice Act require environmental impact reports for state projects that manage forest lands.[38] At least two to three approvals are needed for a controlled burn on California state lands – an air permit, a smoke management plan from the California Air Resources Board or an

air pollution district, and, occasionally, approval from CAL FIRE.[39] Even then, if winds are too still or too strong, the air district can withdraw approval.[40]

The Forest Practice Act (the principal regulatory framework for the management of non-federal forest lands in California[41]) requires approval by CAL FIRE of a Timber Harvesting Plan before the majority of forest management projects can be pursued, which includes the "cutting or removal, or both, of timber."[42] That Timber Harvesting Plan must be reviewed by four agencies – CAL FIRE, the Department of Fish and Wildlife, the Regional Water Quality Control Board, and the California Geological Survey.[43] There are exemptions from the permit requirements, most commonly for the removal of dead or dying trees or for substantially damaged forests.[44] Still, the California Legislative Analyst notes that the rules governing the Forest Practice Act make forest management "prohibitively expensive" for many "small, private landowners, even with an incentive program.[45]

This entire process is too bureaucratic and slow to address our current, urgent needs to mitigate the wildfire risk. For instance, after the Camp Fire destroyed the town of Paradise on Nov. 8, 2018, local officials sought to get approval for forest-thinning projects. But it took two years after the first application for approval for the contract for one of the projects to even go out for bidding. This included 17 months to get final approval from CAL FIRE. Tragically, four days after CAL FIRE's approval, the 2020 North Complex Fire destroyed most of the homes, leaving at least 10 people dead.[46]

Accordingly, new legislation is necessary, which should require a single permit from a single agency for prescribed burns and other thinning methods and which allows for a streamlined process for that purpose.

Exercise the Governor's Emergency Powers

If the Legislature will not cooperate, the governor should exercise his emergency powers to reduce the wildfire peril in those areas where the need is greatest. The governor is authorized to declare a state of emergency based on conditions "of extreme peril to the safety of persons and property," such as fire or drought, which, by reason of their magnitude, are likely beyond the control of any single county or city.[47] During a state of emergency, the governor may suspend any regulatory statute,[48] which would include parts of the Forest Practice Act and CEQA, in order to expedite protective measures.

Other Risk-Reduction Initiatives

The state also needs to hold serious discussions with the logging industry and environmentalists as to how logging companies can assist in thinning densely packed forests near populated communities. Indeed, California's Forest Carbon Plan prepared by CAL FIRE acknowledges that "[f]uel reduction in forests," including through "sustainable commercial timber harvest," can "achieve forest health goals."[49]An added virtue of this approach is that private companies, not the taxpayer, will fund the thinning.

A January 2021 "action plan" from the Governor's Office has instead focused on developing a market for "woody feedstock" and "woody biomass," which otherwise "are piled and burned."[50] But the hope of developing a market over time does not address the urgency of partnering with the private sector today to help thin flammable dense forests. In contrast, in the state of Washington, logging companies have been permitted to cut smaller diameter trees to thin some forests, from which timber can be used to create cross-laminated lumber (lumber that is milled and glued together into beams and lumber boards).[51]

In California, to the extent that cutting smaller trees is less profitable, the logging companies could be given tax credits as an incentive to assist the state in its efforts to thin unhealthy forests.

Some other modest ideas are worth considering:

1. The Governor should urge California's congressional delegation to insist that the U.S. Forest Service dramatically increase the number of acres of federal forest lands that are thinned.

2. Tax incentives or funding should be made available to help homeowners in wildland-urban interfaces upgrade their homes with fire-resistant materials because doing so helps the entire surrounding community. The governor's May Revise does not allocate any funds for this, instead relying on $25 million in the 2020-2021 budget.[52]

3. Reasonable land-use restrictions are also necessary in areas prone to wildfires. Gary Ferguson, the nature and science writer, has observed that, "among the best predictors of property loss in the face of wildfire is whether homes are less than 30 feet apart."[53]

4. The California Council on Science and Technology separately argues in favor of vegetation management and defensible spaces.[54] Thinning vegetation can keep fire on the ground rather than reaching treetops.[55]

Protecting Our Energy Infrastructure

The state's aging energy infrastructure must also be addressed to mitigate the risk of wildfires. Consider that the PG&E equipment that state officials concluded caused the fire that destroyed Paradise was built in 1921.[56] A 2017 presentation prepared for PG&E estimated that its transmission towers were 68 years old on average with a mean life expectancy of 65 years.[57]

And although utility equipment may only be responsible for roughly 10 percent of California wildfires, the LAO notes that "utility power lines caused at least eight of the 20 most destructive fires (40 percent) in California's history" and six of them were sparked since 2015.[58]

To address this risk, the state established a new Wildfire Safety Division in the California Public Utilities Commission in January 2020 to oversee and enforce utilities' compliance with wildfire safety regulations.[59] That division will be transferred to the Office of Energy Infrastructure Safety under the California Natural Resources Agency by July 1, 2021.[60]

That would be a mistake, however. It removes such oversight from the very commission that regulates electric utilities' rates (utilities' income) and their costs. If the state is going to regulate rates, while increasing utilities' costs to achieve ever-increasing amounts of renewable energy, the state needs to consider the costs for any additional safety measures that it imposes upon the utilities. Granting two different agencies responsibility for imposing costs on utilities will undermine an effective effort to strengthen the energy infrastructure.

Moreover, in light of the state's imposition of expensive climate mandates upon utilities – which, in turn, have necessarily diverted resources that could have gone to strengthen their energy infrastructure – the state owes utilities assistance with the additional costs required to harden their energy infrastructure.

After all, reducing the risk of equipment-triggered fires furthers the state's climate goals. As the Nature Conservancy's Christopher Topik notes, while "[f]orestlands … sequester about 13 percent of total U.S. fossil fuel carbon emissions," "projections suggest that forests will become net carbon emitters later this century if steps are not taken to make them more resilient."[61] This includes reducing the risk of equipment-triggered fires.

Fires have also been caused by trees that are too close to, and fall on, transmission lines during storms. For instance, CAL FIRE determined that the 2020 Zogg Fire in Shasta and Tehama Counties, which killed four residents and destroyed over 200 homes, was sparked by a tree (which may have been previously identified for removal) falling on a transmission line. The resulting fire was then fueled by two days of high winds.[62] In turn, the continuing, significant risk of liability from wildfires triggered by utilities' aging equipment has caused utilities to initiate rolling power outages during periods of strong winds. The question is why the state has failed to take greater measures to facilitate the strengthening of the utilities' energy infrastructure and the trimming of trees near power lines, instead of continuing to divert more resources toward achieving escalating climate goals that may have little effect on climate change, particularly when other major countries spew carbon.

Conclusion: 'Nothing in Excess'

The first obligation of government is to protect the public. In the case of climate change, the state cannot place all of its chips on its bet to stop climate change by 2045, while significantly neglecting the ongoing consequences of climate change. Instead, it must balance the cost of further reductions in greenhouse gases against the diversion of resources necessary to both protect against wildfires and strengthen the energy infrastructure. In short, California would do well to acknowledge the wisdom of the ancient Greeks, on whose Temple of Apollo in Delphi was inscribed the maxim, "Nothing in Excess." But California's climate change mandates, like its policies on taxes and regulation, is "everything in excess." It is time to recognize that moderation often achieves more than excess.

Daniel M. Kolkey, an attorney, is a former associate justice of the California Court of Appeal, former counsel to California Governor Pete Wilson, and a member of the board of directors for Pacific Research Institute.

CHAPTER TEN: TOWARD A HEALTHIER CALIFORNIA

CHAPTER TEN
TOWARD A HEALTHIER CALIFORNIA

By Sally Pipes

One of the traditional methods of imposing statism or socialism on a people has been by way of medicine. It's very easy to disguise a medical program as a humanitarian project, most people are a little reluctant to oppose anything that suggests medical care for people who possibly can't afford it.

—*Ronald Reagan*

The U.S. Senate, on March 18, 2021, confirmed California's own Xavier Becerra as Secretary of Health and Human Services.[1] Though he has no executive or healthcare experience, it's hardly surprising that President Joe Biden chose him to be his administration's top health policy official.

Becerra has been a staunch advocate for Obamacare. As California Attorney General, he led an effort by 20 states and the District of Columbia to defend the Affordable Care Act against an attempt by the Trump administration and more than a dozen states to overturn the law in the courts.[2]

He'd prefer even more government in health care. In 2017, Becerra boasted that he'd "been a supporter of Medicare for All for the 24 years" he represented a Los Angeles-area district in Congress.[3]

Becerra now says he supports President Biden's plan to build on the Affordable Care Act. But he may still be able to indulge his single-payer dreams.

As HHS Secretary, Becerra has the power to grant waivers that could allow states to implement their own single-payer systems.[4] The Golden State has long flirted with the idea. With a Californian in Washington, progressive activists think the time may be ripe for a government takeover of the state's health insurance system.

Few state governments have a greater presence in their healthcare market than California's does. All that intervention has led to spiraling costs and declining outcomes for those unfortunate enough to rely on the state for coverage.

It's time for a different approach. Less regulation, freer markets, and greater choice are what it will take to secure higher-quality care at lower cost in California.

The Unstoppable Growth of Medi-Cal

California's Medicaid program, dubbed Medi-Cal, is the primary vehicle by which the state has expanded its hold on the state's health sector. More than 13 million people get coverage through the program – about one-third of the state's population.[5]

Covering them is not cheap. In 2021-22, spending on Medi-Cal will top $120 billion, according to February 2021 projections from the nonpartisan California Legislative Analyst's Office (LAO). That's almost three times what the program spent in 2012-13.[6]

Spending has increased because the program has grown substantially. The state added about 3.7 million people to Medi-Cal under the terms of the Affordable Care Act, which opened the program to anyone making up to 138 percent of the poverty level starting in 2014.[7] The state Department of Health Care Services reports that Medi-Cal enrollment grew by 4.5 million, or nearly 60 percent, between December 2012 and December 2014.[8]

That's not enough for Gov. Gavin Newsom, who has pushed to expand Medi-Cal further. In June 2019, Newsom signed a state budget that included a plan to cover undocumented immigrants between the ages of 19 and 25.[9] The state earmarked $375 million in 2020 for Medi-Cal coverage for this group.[10]

As of December 2020, Medi-Cal covered about 200,000 undocumented immigrant children and young adults. The new budget provides $1.3 billion in funding to expand the program to older undocumented immigrants.[11] Previous estimates say it could cost the state some $2.6 billion, according to a 2020 report by the Legislative Analyst's Office.[12]

As Medi-Cal grows, beneficiaries have a harder time accessing coverage. Doctors generally limit the number of Medi-Cal patients they see because the program's reimbursements are so low.[13] Expanding the program further will increase competition among beneficiaries for an already limited number of appointments.

New Taxes, Higher Premiums, Bigger Problems

To help pay for all this state-sponsored coverage, California requires all state residents to secure health insurance or pay a fine of $750 or 2.5 percent of their household income, whichever is greater.[14] The state projects the mandate will bring in $1 billion over three years.[15]

This state-level individual mandate took effect in 2020, two years after the Trump administration zeroed out the federal penalty for violating Obamacare's individual mandate.[16] [17]

The annual premium for the average benchmark plan on the Covered California exchange was over $5,100 in 2021.[18] Annual deductibles can be thousands more. So, a person could have to spend five figures on health care before he gets a dollar from his insurance company.

Rather than try to bring down the cost of coverage, California just throws more taxpayer money at the problem. Starting in 2020, the state offered subsidized coverage through the exchange to people making up to 600 percent of the federal poverty level.[19] That's $75,000 a year for an individual and more than $154,000 for a family of four.[20] The Affordable Care Act only offered subsidies to people making up to 400 percent of poverty.

But as California goes, so goes the nation. President Biden's 2021 American Rescue Plan Act followed California's example and extended insurance subsidies to the well-off by capping premiums for those who make more than 400 percent of the poverty level at 8.5 percent of income.[21]

Progressives Hope for a State Takeover

Many progressives hope that expanding Medicaid and lavishing subsidies on exchange shoppers are but a prelude to a government takeover of the state's health insurance system.

It wouldn't be their first try. In 2017, California's state Senate voted to advance SB 562, the Healthy California Act, which would have established a single-payer system in the state.[22]

An analysis from the state Senate concluded that the bill would cost $400 billion – double the state's entire budget.[23] Half of that total was to come from existing Medicare and Medicaid funding. Generating the rest would have required the likes of a new 15 percent payroll tax.[24]

California Assembly Speaker Anthony Rendon broke with his fellow Democrats and shelved what he called the "woefully incomplete" bill, given that the legislation – something that would have cast aside the entire private healthcare system – was offered little more than a general blueprint. But that was not the end of California's single-payer saga.[25]

In December 2019, Newsom convened a group of healthcare providers and health policy wonks to explore how to implement a state-level single-payer system.[26] The Healthy California For All Commission met for the first time on Jan. 27, 2020 and was supposed to deliver its final report by Feb. 2021.[27]

That report was delayed by the COVID-19 pandemic. But progressive lawmakers aren't bothering to wait for it. In February 2021, a group of California Democrats introduced AB 1400, the Guaranteed Health Care For All Act.[28]

Like the Healthy California Act, AB 1400 would initiate a government takeover of the state's health-insurance sector. It would dissolve Medicare, Medi-Cal, and private health insurance and dump all residents of the Golden State into a new, government-run health plan called CalCare.[29]

On April 21, 2021, Assembly member Ash Kalra, one of the sponsors of AB 1400, announced that the bill would be shelved until later in the legislative session. Observers speculated that the lack of a clear funding source was a sticking point.[30]

The goal of any health reform effort should be to deliver better value for every dollar we spend on care. Ever-greater levels of government spending have led to diminishing returns at massive cost to taxpayers. It's time for a different approach, one that leverages the power of markets to produce higher-quality care at lower cost.

Setting the Stage for Market-Based Solutions

Lawmakers can start by rolling back bloated healthcare programs and repealing the taxes that support them, starting with Medi-Cal.

Ideally, California would return Medi-Cal eligibility to pre-2014 levels. A more realistic goal might be to roll back the expansion of Medi-Cal benefits to undocumented immigrants aged 19-25.

Doing so would reduce competition for scarce appointments and thereby make it easier for beneficiaries who are legal residents to access care. And it would discourage undocumented people from flocking to California for free health care.

Shrinking Medi-Cal would also reduce Californians' tax burden. That would help the entirety of the state's economy, not just the healthcare space.

More than 650,000 people fled California in 2019, thanks in no small part to the state's burdensome tax regime.[31] [32] Reducing the size of the program that eats up billions in tax revenue would allow state leaders to cut taxes – and thereby keep productive people from leaving.

A smaller Medi-Cal could also reduce premiums for the privately insured. The program pays healthcare providers bargain-basement rates that sometimes don't even cover their costs. To compensate, doctors and hospitals charge private insurers more. If the share of their patient load covered by Medi-Cal declines, then they won't have to shift as many costs onto private insurers – and will have the flexibility to reduce their rates. Those reductions will flow through to consumers in the form of lower premiums.

Lower taxes and less government spending will create conditions conducive to job creation. That's exactly the kind of environment present and former Medi-Cal beneficiaries need. It's far better for them, for taxpayers, and for the economy if they're able to get decent jobs that provide health insurance benefits – or give them the income they need to purchase it on their own.

California had the fourth-highest unemployment rate in the country, as of February 2021.[33] Without significant action, that will not change. Government is strangling the state's economy, creating a land of haves and have-nots. Getting residents back to work will reduce strain on government coffers and stimulate the economy.

To make life even more affordable for average Californians, the state can repeal its individual mandate, which simply penalizes those who can't afford health insurance or have decided it's not worth the five-figure yearly expense.

Expanding Coverage Options, Reducing Premium Costs

After state lawmakers roll back harmful regulations, they can begin implementing effective market-oriented reforms.

Right off the bat, lawmakers can repeal SB 910 and allow the sale of short-term health plans.[34] Short-term plans can last up to a year, can be renewed for up to three years, and are not subject to Obamacare's panoply of rules and regulations.[35] That's why the average short-term plan costs 80 percent less than an unsubsidized exchange plan, according to a 2019 analysis from eHealth.[36]

Democrats have long derided short-term plans as "junk insurance" and sought to restrict their sale. But as research from the Manhattan Institute's Chris Pope has demonstrated, these plans often provide access to broader physician networks than comparable exchange plans, usually at a fraction of the price.[37]

One study found that more than 600,000 people would buy short-term plans if California lifted its ban. That would reduce the state's uninsured population by 200,000.[38]

Short-term plans don't just benefit those who purchase them. They drive down premiums across the board by increasing competition and marketplace diversity. According to research published by the Galen Institute, premiums for benchmark plans on the exchanges declined by 7.9 percent between 2018 and 2021 in states that permitted the sale of short-term plans. In states that restricted their sale, benchmark premiums dropped just 3.2 percent.[39]

California should also green-light the sale of association health plans, which allow small businesses and self-employed workers in the same industry to band together to form an "association" and purchase health coverage like a large employer.[40] [41] Like short-term plans, association health plans are exempt from Obamacare's mandates – and so have the flexibility to tailor affordable coverage to the needs of their members.[42]

Free Doctors, Healthy Patients

There are several ways the state can reform its provider market to make care more affordable, too.

To be fair, the Golden State gets a number of things right on this front. California does not have certificate-of-need laws, which require healthcare providers to obtain government approval before offering new services, constructing new facilities, and more.[43] Data from the Kaiser Family Foundation show that per-capita health expenditures are 11 percent higher in states with certificate-of-need laws than in states without them.[44]

California also seems headed in the right direction on scope-of-practice laws. The state recently enacted legislation that allows nurse practitioners to practice without physician supervision.[45]

The United States currently has 290,000 nurse practitioners, 90 percent of whom specialize in primary care.[46] Nurse practitioners hold graduate degrees, have advanced medical training, and have prescribing privileges in all 50 states and the District of Columbia.[47] [48] Allowing these highly-credentialed medical professionals to practice on their own will relieve overburdened doctors and improve patient access to care.

California still prevents physician assistants from practicing without physician oversight, even though they, like nurse practitioners, have the requisite training and education.[49] Giving physician assistants greater freedom to practice would reduce pressure on the state's health system and help clinicians and patients alike.

State licensing laws for health professionals are due for review, too.

California is not a party to the Interstate Medical Licensure Compact, which allows doctors licensed in 29 states and the District of Columbia to practice freely in the other states covered by the Compact.[50] Recognizing medical licenses issued in other states would allow California to expand its physician supply and help improve access to care, especially in underserved areas.

Nurse practitioners face similar licensing barriers. In a 2021 essay published by the *Los Angeles Daily News*, Karin Lips of the Network of Enlightened Women shared the story of an NP who had moved to California with her husband, who served in the military. It took more than six months and more than $1,000 in fees for the woman, who was licensed in Florida, to gain permission to work in California.[51] Lawmakers have introduced legislation to rectify that situation, but it has failed to move forward.

In March 2020, Governor Newsom signed an executive order streamlining medical licensure rules in response to the COVID-19 pandemic. These waivers made it easier for physicians to renew licenses that would soon expire and for retired physicians in good standing to reactivate dormant licenses.[52]

These are smart policies, and not just in times of emergency.

Embracing the Telehealth Revolution

Relaxed licensure requirements would also allow Californians to take full advantage of the telehealth revolution.

As part of its pandemic response, California made it easier for patients to consult with out-of-state physicians over Skype, Zoom or FaceTime.[53] Reimbursement structures were also altered, so doctors received the same amount for telehealth visits as in-person visits.[54]

Equalizing reimbursements encourages doctors to offer a wider array of telehealth services and makes it easier for patients to "visit" their doctors from the comfort of their homes.

The potential benefits for patients are endless. Those who struggle to walk or get around can still get the care they need. Those who live in remote parts of the state can gain access to top-notch specialists across California – or across the country.

Increased telehealth access can also save money. According to a 2017 Health Affairs study, the average telehealth visit cost just $79, compared to $146 for an in-person visit.[55]

Transparency, Competition, Savings

To maximize the benefits of these proposals, lawmakers should inject some much-needed price transparency into California's healthcare space.

Beginning in 2021, the Centers for Medicare and Medicaid Services required hospitals nationwide to publish their previously secret prices.[56] This was a big win for patients. Efficient markets can drive down healthcare costs more effectively than any government regulation. But markets can only function when consumers have access to prices and can shop around for the best deal.

Without transparency, providers can effectively charge whatever they want and profit off the opacity. There's no good reason why one expectant mother in California should pay $15,000 for a Cesarean section – and another pay $40,000.[57]

Going forward, hospitals will have to offer a consumer-friendly list of prices for 300 shoppable services, which accounted for around 43 percent of out-of-pocket health spending in 2017.[58] [59] There's evidence from California that price transparency in the healthcare market can yield lower costs.

In 2011, the California Public Employees' Retirement System, or CalPERS, identified several hospitals that could provide high-quality hip and knee replacement surgeries for $30,000.[60] Beneficiaries could opt to undergo a more expensive surgery at a different hospital – but would have to pay the difference out of pocket.[61]

Unsurprisingly, patients chose the cheaper hospitals, which saw their market share increase by 28 percent.[62] As more expensive hospitals began losing business, they reduced their prices. Competition spurred by this "reference pricing" system cut prices of hip and knee replacement surgeries by more than 20 percent, saving CalPERS $6 million over two years.[63]

California can further stoke competition by authorizing shared savings programs, which allows patients who shop for the best-value care to share in any savings they generate for their insurer.[64] Such efforts will encourage patients to shop around for care and ensure that cost-cutting reforms directly benefit patients.

Important Points to Consider as We Tackle Reform

First, Medi-Cal is the biggest driver of healthcare costs and inefficiencies in California. Any reform effort must begin by reining in the program.

Second, solving California's healthcare problems will require fewer government mandates and subsidies, not more – and certainly not a single-payer system.

Third, it's time for California to allow the sale of short-term and association health plans, which provide affordable coverage options and drive down premiums for everyone.

Fourth, California deserves credit for regulating the practice of medicine relatively lightly. But the state can do more to create a freer healthcare labor market.

Fifth, California has seen firsthand how price transparency and competition can drive down health costs and needs to find ways – even around the margins – to incorporate these concepts in its healthcare policies.

The Golden State Model

Government has failed to deliver high-quality care at affordable prices in California. Yet many of the state's leaders want to inject more government into the healthcare system by making the state the lone insurer.

If that happens, Californians will face long waits, rationed care, a doctor shortage and higher taxes. That's the reality in Canada, where the government has a monopoly on covering everything it deems medically necessary. I know firsthand – I was born there.

It's time for a new approach – one that relies on markets to improve quality and reduce cost in the health sector, just as they have in every other sector of the economy.

Sally Pipes is president and CEO of the Pacific Research Institute.

CONCLUSION: A BLUEPRINT FOR REFORM

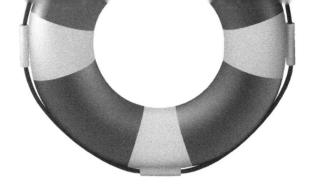

CONCLUSION
A BLUEPRINT FOR REFORM

Steven Greenhut

There has always been something slightly bipolar about California. It was either utopia or dystopia, a dream or a nightmare, a hope or a broken promise – and too infrequently anything in between.

—*Kevin Starr,*
the late California historian

Since the Gold Rush popularized the idea of California as the Golden State – a place of instant wealth and endless possibilities – Californians have alternately bemoaned the impending collapse of the California Dream. Such disappointments really did start shortly after the 49ers headed from across the globe to find fortune in our state's goldfields.

"As the mining region grew more crowded, there was less gold to go around," explained PBS' The *American Experience*. "As the surface gold disappeared, individual miners found their dreams of cashing in on the gold rush growing more elusive. Many men went to work for the larger mining companies that invested in technology and equipment to reach the gold that lay below the surface. By the mid-1850s mining for gold had become less an individual enterprise and more a wage labor job."

That perhaps was the first big California disappointment, born out of unrealistic expectations about what life here would mean. Likewise, the post-World War II visions of California – a suburban house surrounded by palm trees, Hollywood glitter, wide freeways to drive shiny new cars and a boisterous surf culture – soon degraded into complaints about traffic, urban sprawl, untrammeled immigration and widening poverty. Most of us have experienced both sides of the California experience.

In recent decades, conservative-minded Californians have bemoaned the state's political shift from the land of Ronald Reagan to a state where Republican gubernatorial candidates struggle to garner 40 percent of the vote. Every statewide constitutional office is now held by a Democrat, with Democrats holding supermajorities in both houses of the Legislature. That certainly limits the chances that market-oriented reforms will take hold.

As earlier chapters have noted, progressives now see California as a place where they can try out their political and social experiments – in the hopes that their visions can become the model for the nation. That often has meant a focus on social engineering rather than, say, transportation engineering. Too often, progressive lawmakers have been more intent on implementing their ideologically driven nostrums than in tending to the nuts-and-bolts of running the state. For their part, Republicans have failed to offer an alternative vision and have stuck with their old approach – championing stale "law and order" themes and ignoring the state's changing politics and demographics – and have been happy enough winning a minority of safe legislative seats in shrinking GOP areas.

This book has detailed some of the results of that shift in public policy. For the first time in more than a century, California's population actually has declined. A steady stream of news stories detail the out-migration of mostly middle-class Californians to Texas and other states. Even California's big technology firms, the engine of the state's economy and budget, have been moving their headquarters or expanding operations elsewhere.

As Starr's quotation above notes, this has led to a certain pessimistic thinking. One need only read conservative media to see California depicted as a dystopia, where throngs of homeless have overtaken San Francisco, criminals run rampant on the streets, and before congestion and poverty rates have turned our once-vibrant suburbs into a third-world hellhole. Those of us who live here know that's far from the truth, although we're not naïve about the depth of the problems the state now faces – or the degree to which some urban neighborhoods have become borderline anarchic.

The goal of this book is not to change via political organizing and the like, but to detail some fundamental reforms that California politicians from either party can embrace. California is likely to remain a Democratic bastion for the remainder of our lives, but that's no reason to give up hope of building a more practical and reform-minded political consensus.

After all, many of the state's finest modern achievements – from building its modern freeway system to harnessing its water resources to creating what was once the nation's most formidable public-education system – were accomplished under the leadership of Democratic governors Earl Warren and Pat Brown. Even Jerry Brown, in his last two terms as governor, championed a traditional form of liberalism that often was open to reformist ideas. California's current Democrats could potentially return to the party's good-government roots without giving up their more pie-in-the-sky objectives.

Likewise, the California Republican Party, despite its dismal election prospects and falling registration levels, could realistically revive itself – or at least pull back from the brink – by embracing the types of practical, quality-of-life-improving reforms that are detailed in this book. A little balance is in order and Lord knows California could benefit from some heightened political competition, a lot less partisanship, and some fresh thinking about new ideas.

This book doesn't cover every one of the state's challenges, of course. It doesn't delve into seemingly insurmountable political challenges, either. For instance, California's public-sector unions thwart every manner of reform – from education to road building to finances – given their outsized political power. That, ultimately, is a political problem that is beyond this book's scope.

Here is a summary of the general suggestions from the authors of the previous chapters – sound ideas that politicians from either party can at least theoretically embrace. Please refer back to the individual chapters for details, but these are some key takeaways:

- The state should consider a wide-ranging tax rebate program to lure large-scale investments into poor areas such as south Los Angeles and the Central Valley.
- California should stop the climate virtue signaling and instead embrace growth-oriented environmental policies.
- The state needs to reform the California Environmental Quality Act (CEQA), which makes it too easy for anti-growth groups or unions seeking to hobble competitors file lawsuits that delay or even stop needed housing projects.
- The state needs to overhaul its tax system and provide incentives to create jobs and housing. The current system is too reliant on sales taxes at a time when much of brick-and-mortar retail is collapsing.

California's Housing Crisis – Wendell Cox

- The Legislature should create a "Housing Opportunity Area" (HOA) in the interior to restore the competitive market for land, thereby preventing further deterioration in housing affordability.
- The HOA would include the San Joaquin and Sacramento valley counties from Shasta to Kern, as well as San Bernardino, Riverside and Imperial and Antelope Valley in Los Angeles County.
- Like the CEQA streamlining authorized for subsidized low-income housing in Senate Bill 7, such zoning and land-use regulatory streamlining would apply to middle-income and low-income greenfield projects. Authorization would be virtually automatic for developments of, say, at least 50-plus houses or apartments that would be served by infrastructure (public or private).
- Impact fee reform: The state needs to identify means to finance new development from general revenue sources, not new owners and apartment dwellers.

- The state needs to embrace policies that make California a more affordable place to live.
- The Legislature needs to improve the efficiency of homeless services by empowering nonprofits and better leveraging state resources.
- California should repeal or reform harmful policy changes like Proposition 47, which reduced penalties for various property crimes routinely committed by homeless people – thus removing prosecutors' ability to push people into rehabilitation programs.
- The state should create more homeless courts that are better able to address the issues afflicting this unique population.

Decongesting our Roads and Freeways – Adrian Moore

- California must make infrastructure a priority. The Legislature likes to talk about how important infrastructure is when they put a multibillion-dollar bond measure on the ballot for voters to approve. But they pay little to no attention to how well the money is used, how to get the most out of it, or if their spending is effective.
- The state needs to prioritize projects based on impact and benefits. Given limited resources, it is vital to steer money to the projects that are the most important and will provide the greatest public benefit.
- The state also needs to address political and management barriers. For decades, infrastructure stakeholders in California have pointed out that permitting processes seem more designed to deny projects than to approve them.
- It's time to focus on the long-term life cycle of projects, not just this legislative session. Infrastructure lasts a long time, providing benefits to users for many years. This is why it can make sense to borrow money to build it – in future years while making payments on the debt, users are also enjoying the benefits of what it built.

- State officials need to recognize that only 10 percent of the state's water is used for commercial and residential purposes and move away from a conservation-only approach to water resources.
- California needs to upgrade and expand its water infrastructure system, so that it can store more water in wet years for use in dry ones.
- The state needs to reduce its regulatory hurdles that impede the construction of desalination and private water projects.
- The state needs to fix the Delta conveyance system, promote water recycling, improving its water pricing and trading system, and embrace a policy of abundance rather than scarcity.

A Return to Educational Excellence – Lance Izumi

- Regular public schools should emulate charter schools and re-open in fall 2021 to full five-day-a-week in-person instruction.
- Anti-charter-school laws such as AB 1505 should be repealed and the Legislature should reject the new anti-charter-school bills that are making their way through the Legislature.
- The state needs to offer a positive pro-charter-school agenda based on the model legislation proposed by organizations such as the National Alliance of Public Charter Schools.
- Private groups should support efforts to encourage teachers to opt out of their unions. Furthermore, policymakers should look beyond charter schools to other school choice tools such as education savings accounts. Other states are implementing such choice programs and California's leaders should learn from their example.

Arresting California's Crime Problem – Pat Nolan

- The California Department of Corrections and Rehabilitation needs to focus parole officers on offenders who pose the greatest threat. As one report noted, "California's parole system is so overburdened that parolees who represent a serious public safety risk are not watched closely enough, and those who wish to go straight cannot get the help they need."

- Prisoners should be protected from assaults inside prison. No crime, no matter how heinous, includes being beaten and raped as part of the sentence. Since the government prevents inmates from defending themselves, it is incumbent on the government to protect them.
- Cases should be decided individually, not as an assembly line. The harm done by a sentence should never be greater than the harm caused by the crime.
- Prisons should make a priority of matching inmates with mentors, responsible members of the community, who can help inmates prepare a life plan to stay out of trouble when they return to the community.

Building a Sustainable Budget – Richard Mersereau

- California needs to implement "best practices" from other states, as well as from our own local governments, which can result in significant cost savings in all areas of government.
- The governor and Legislature should undertake a comprehensive review of all regulations affecting private businesses and professions, as well as taxpayer-funded services.
- The state needs to embrace a Governor's Reorganization Plan (GRP) that enables agency and department consolidation, streamlining and, as the name suggests, reorganization to promote a better and more-efficient budget process.
- Lawmakers must play by the rules. For instance, both houses of the Legislature must ensure that every bill will receive a full and fair hearing upon the request of the author.

California Burning: Wildfires and Climate Change – Daniel Kolkey

- The governor should urge California's congressional delegation to insist that the U.S. Forest Service dramatically increase the number of acres of federal forest lands that are thinned.
- Tax incentives or funding should be made available to help homeowners in wildland-urban interfaces upgrade their homes with fire-resistant materials because doing so helps the entire surrounding community.

- Reasonable land-use restrictions are also necessary in areas prone to wildfires. Gary Ferguson, the nature and science writer, has observed that, "among the best predictors of property loss in the face of wildfire is whether homes are less than 30 feet apart."
- The California Council on Science and Technology separately argues in favor of vegetation management and defensible spaces. Thinning vegetation can keep fire on the ground rather than reaching treetops.

Toward a Healthier California – Sally Pipes

- Medi-Cal is the biggest driver of healthcare costs and inefficiencies in California, so any reform effort must begin by reining in the program.
- Solving California's healthcare problems will require fewer government mandates and subsidies, not more – and certainly not a single-payer system.
- It's time for California to allow the sale of short-term and association health plans, which provide affordable coverage options and drive down premiums for everyone.
- California deserves credit for regulating the practice of medicine relatively lightly. But the state can do more to create a freer healthcare labor market.
- California has seen firsthand how price transparency and competition can drive down health costs, so it should expand on that policy.

ENDNOTES

Chapter 1

1   Laura Tyson and Lenny Mendonca, "The Birthplace of America's New Progressive Era," *Project Syndicate*, Feb. 18, 2019, https://www.project-syndicate.org/commentary/california-federalism-new-progressive-era-by-laura-tyson-and-lenny-mendonca-2019-02.

2   Steve Kettmann, "The Californization of America," *New York Times*, June 2, 2018, https://www.nytimes.com/2018/06/02/opinion/sunday/california-progressive-politics.html.

3   Evan Halper, "Make America California Again? That's California's Plan," *Los Angeles Times*, Jan. 17, 2021, https://www.latimes.com/politics/story/2021-01-17/make-america-california-again-how-biden-will-try.

4   Dan Walters, California still No. 1 in poverty, *CalMatters*, Sept. 17, 2019, https://calmatters.org/commentary/2019/09/high-cost-california-no-1-in-poverty/.

5   Spencer P. Morrison, "California's Income Inequality Now Worse Than Mexico's; Poverty Level Highest In America," *National Economics*, Jan. 17, 2018, https://nationaleconomicseditorial.com/2018/01/17/californian-income-inequality-tops-mexico/.

6   Ethan Rarick, *California Rising: The Life and Times of Pat Brown*, University of California Press, (Berkeley, CA: 2005), p. 383. https://www.ucpress.edu/book/9780520248281/california-rising.

7   Staff, "California Economy: Annual Forecast Charts," California Lutheran University Center for Economic Research and Forecasting, Sept. 14, 2017, https://blogs.callutheran.edu/cerf/files/2017/09/Annual_Pop_PerCapitaGDP_Forecast1.pdf.

8   Joel Kotkin and Marshall Toplansky, "California Feudalism: The Squeeze on the Middle Class," Chapman University Center for Demographics and Policy, 2018, https://www.chapman.edu/wilkinson/_files/Feudalism.pdf.

9   David Friedman and Jennifer Hernandez, "California, Greenhouse Gas Regulation and Climate Change," Chapman University Center for Demographics and Policy," 2018, https://www.newgeography.com/content/006014-california-greenhouse-gas-regulation-and-climate-change.

10 Mark Nelson and Michael Shellenberger, "Electricity prices in California rose three times more in 2017 than they did in the rest of the United States," *Environmental Progress*, Feb. 12, 2018, http://environmentalprogress.org/big-news/2018/2/12/electricity-prices-rose-three-times-more-in-california-than-in-rest-of-us-in-2017.

11   Competitive Enterprise Institute analysis, "10 Year Job Growth: 2009 – 2019, https://app.powerbi.com/view?r=eyJrIjoiOTg4ODE4OGYtYmVmMS00ZTF-hLTg1MjQtMzc4ODUwODQ2OTM4IiwidCI6ImY2OGI2ZDZjLWIyMjItNGQ-wYS1hZjc0LTVlNGEwMGFkMzVkZCIsImMiOjN9.

12 "State Unemployment Rates," National Conference of State Legislatures, March 2021, https://www.ncsl.org/research/labor-and-employment/state-unemployment-update.aspx.

13   "Unemployment Rates for Metropolitan Areas," U.S. Bureau of Labor Statistics, accessed June 20, 2021, https://www.bls.gov/web/metro/laummtrk.htm.

14   Brian Addison, "Trio of New Studies Show Low Income, Middle Class Are Vacating California While Wealthy Move In; Housing Costs to Blame," *Long Beach Post*, May 3, 2018, https://lbpost.com/longbeachize/trio-new-studies-show-low-income-middle-class-vacating-california-wealthy-move-housing-costs-blame.

15   Kelsey Thomas, "Adios, California: Thousands of homebuyers flocking to Las Vegas for 'American Dream'," KSNV, July 16, 2018, http://news3lv.com/news/local/adios-california-thousands-of-homebuyers-flocking-to-las-vegas-for-american-dream.

16   William H. Frey, "How migration of millennials and seniors has shifted since the Great Recession," Brookings Institution, Jan. 31, 2019, https://www.brookings.edu/research/how-migration-of-millennials-and-seniors-has-shifted-since-the-great-recession/.

17   Joel Kotkin and Wendell Cox, "Fading Promise: Millennial Prospects in the Golden State," Chapman University Center for Demographics and Policy, 2017, https://www.chapman.edu/wilkinson/_files/cdp-fading-inside.pdf.

18   American Enterprise Institute, "Best and Worst Metro Areas to Be a First-time Homebuyer," 2019, https://www.aei.org/best-and-worst-metro-areas-to-be-a-first-time-homebuyer/.

19   Ibid.

20   Steve Rubenstein, "California birthrate plunges to lowest level in a century," *San Francisco Chronicle*, May 17, 2018, https://www.sfchronicle.com/bayarea/article/California-birthrate-plunges-to-lowest-level-in-a-12923521.php.

21   Gary Becker and Richard Posner, "Low Birth Rates: Causes, Consequences, and Remedies," The Becker-Posner Blog, Aug. 18, 2013, http://www.becker-posner-blog.com/2013/08/low-birth-rates-causes-consequences-and-remedies-becker.html.

22   Wendell Cox, "California Population Lags Behind Projections," *New Geography*, Aug. 24, 2017, http://www.newgeography.com/content/005723-california-population-lags-behind-projections.

23   Margot Adler, "My '70s Show — Remembering 'Ecotopia' Author Ernest Callenbach," National Public Radio, https://www.npr.org/2012/04/28/151543517/my-70s-show-remembering-ecotopia-author-ernest-callenbach#:~:text=His%201975%20cult%2Dclassic%2C%20Ecotopia,million%20copies%20in%20many%20languages.

24   "Progress Cleaning the Air and Improving People's Health," U.S. Environmental Protection Agency, accessed June 20, 2021, https://www.epa.gov/clean-air-act-overview/progress-cleaning-air-and-improving-peoples-health.

25   Andrew Tarantola, "California to ban sale of new gas-powered vehicles by 2035," *Engadget,* Sept. 23, 2020, https://www.engadget.com/california-to-ban-sale-of-new-gaspowered-cars-by-2035-180313529.html.

26   David Friedman and Jennifer Hernandez, "California, Greenhouse Gas Regulation and Climate Change," Chapman University Center for Demographics and Policy," 2018, https://www.newgeography.com/content/006014-california-greenhouse-gas-regulation-and-climate-change.

27   Robert Bryce, "The High Cost of California Electricity Is Increasing Poverty," Foundation for Research on Equal Opportunity, July 8, 2020, https://freopp. org/the-high-cost-of-california-electricity-is-increasing-poverty-d7bc4021b705.

28   Wendell Cox, "Los Angeles Transit Ridership Losses Lead National Decline," *New Geography*, Nov. 15, 2017, https://www.newgeography.com/content/005800-los-angeles-transit-ridership-losses-lead-national-decline.

29   David Friedman and Jennifer Hernandez, "California, Greenhouse Gas Regulation and Climate Change," Chapman University Center for Demographics and Policy," 2018, https://www.newgeography.com/content/006014-california-greenhouse-gas-regulation-and-climate-change.

30   "Struggling to Stay Afloat: The Real Cost Measure in California," United Ways of California, 2019, https://www.unitedwaysca.org/realcost.

31   Staff, "Is California the welfare capital?" *The San Diego Union-Tribune*, July 28, 2012, http://www.sandiegouniontribune.com/news/politics/sdut-welfare-capital-of-the-us-2012jul28-htmlstory.html.

32   Sal Rodriguez, "Progressive California's disgraceful child poverty problem," *Long Beach Press-Telegram*, July 23, 2018, https://www.presstelegram. com/2018/07/23/progressive-californias-disgraceful-child-poverty-problem/.

33   "America's Shrinking Middle Class: A Close Look at Changes Within Metropolitan Areas," Pew Research Center, 2016, https://www.pewresearch.org/social-trends/2016/05/11/americas-shrinking-middle-class-a-close-look-at-changes-within-metropolitan-areas/.

34   Matt Levin, "California's rich-poor gap: The reality may surprise you," *CalMatters*, June 23, 2020, https://calmatters.org/articles/income-inequality-in-california-may-not-look-like-you-think-it-does-and-why-that-may-be-a-good-thing/.

35   Emma G. Gallegos, "Los Angeles is the Poorest Big City," *LAist*, Sept. 19, 2014, http://laist.com/2014/09/19/los_angeles_is_the_poorest_of_the_m.php.

36   Kalima Rose and Judith Bell, "Expanding Opportunity: New Resources to Meet California's Housing Needs," *Policy Link*, Winter 2005, http://www.policylink.org/sites/default/files/HousingCalifornia_final.pdf; http://newsroom. ucla.edu/stories/ucla-study-identifies-l-a-as-most-unaffordable-rental-market-in-the-nation.

37   Ian Schwartz, "Kamala Harris On Immigration: Sessions Wants To Roll Back The Clock, 'California Represents The Future,'" *RealClearPolitics*, March 8, 2018, https://www.realclearpolitics.com/video/2018/03/08/kamala_harris_on_immigration_sessions_wants_to_roll_back_the_clock_california_represents_the_future_.html.

38   Emily Benedek, "California is Cleansing Jews from History," *Tablet*, Jan, 27, 2021, https://www.tabletmag.com/sections/news/articles/california-ethnic-studies-curriculum.

39   David Friedman and Jennifer Hernandez, "California, Greenhouse Gas Regulation and Climate Change," Chapman University Center for Demographics and Policy," 2018, https://www.newgeography.com/content/006014-california-greenhouse-gas-regulation-and-climate-change.

40 Kalima Rose and Judith Bell, "Expanding Opportunity: New Resources to Meet California's Housing Needs," *Policy Link*, Winter 2005, http://www.policylink.org/sites/default/files/HousingCalifornia_final.pdf; http://newsroom.ucla.edu/stories/ucla-study-identifies-l-a-as-most-unaffordable-rental-market-in-the-nation.

41 Ibid.

42 Staff, "California Earns a C on State Report Card, Ranks 32nd in Nation," *Education Week*, Jan. 17, 2018, https://www.edweek.org/leadership/california-earns-a-c-on-state-report-card-ranks-32nd-in-nation/2018/01.

43 Niall McCarthy, "2020 Saw Unprecedented Murder Spike In Major U.S. Cities," *Statista*, Jan. 12, 2021, https://www.statista.com/chart/23905/change-in-homicides-in-us-cities/.

44 Antonio Garcia Martinez, "How Silicon Valley Fuels an Informal Caste System," *Wired*, July 9, 2018, https://www.wired.com/story/how-silicon-valley-fuels-an-informal-caste-system/.

45 Adam Beam, "California measure aims to pay off 80% of most unpaid rent," Associated Press, Jan. 25, 2021, https://apnews.com/article/legislature-coronavirus-pandemic-california-gavin-newsom-state-legislature-7180696ef98110ed0ec80b932a2d24d3.

46 Gregory Ferenstein, "The Disruptors," *City Journal*, Winter 2017, https://www.city-journal.org/html/disrupters-14950.html.

47 Gregory Ferenstein, "A Lot of Billionaires Are Giving to Democrats. Here's a Look at their Agenda," *Forbes*, February 26, 2016, https://www.forbes.com/sites/gregoryferenstein/2016/02/26/a-lot-of-billionaires-are-giving-to-democrats-heres-a-data-driven-look-at-their-agenda/#2002ef134869; Todd Haselton, "Mark Zuckerberg joins Silicon Valley bigwigs in calling for government to give everybody free money," *Yahoo!*, May 25, 2017, https://finance.yahoo.com/news/mark-zuckerberg-joins-silicon-valley-202800717.html; Patrick Gillespie, "Mark Zuckerberg supports universal basic income. What is it?" CNN, May 6, 2017, https://money.cnn.com/2017/05/26/news/economy/mark-zuckerberg-universal-basic-income/index.html; Chris Weller, "Elon Musk doubles down on universal basic income: 'It's going to be necessary'," *Business Insider*, February 13, 2017, https://www.businessinsider.com/elon-musk-universal-basic-income-2017-2.

48 Joel Kotkin and Marshall Toplansky, "Who Will Control the 21st Century? Whoever Controls Space," *Newsweek*, April 16, 2021, https://www.newsweek.com/who-will-control-21st-century-whoever-controls-space-opinion-1584024.

49 John Shinal, "Silicon Valley's quirky politics recall the railroad boom of pre-Civil War America: Study, CNBC, Sept. 9, 2017, https://www.cnbc.com/2017/09/09/stanford-study-on-silicon-valley-politics-finds-roots-in-19th-century.html.

50 Mark Baldassare, Dean Bonner, Alyssa Dykman and Rachel Lawler, "Californians and Their Government," Public Policy Institute of California, September 2019, https://www.ppic.org/wp-content/uploads/ppic-statewide-survey-californians-and-their-government-september-2019.pdf.

51 Alissa J. Rubin, "Macron Inspects Damage After 'Yellow Vest' Protests as France Weighs State of Emergency," *The New York Times*, Dec. 1, 2018, https://www.nytimes.com/2018/12/01/world/europe/france-yellow-vests-protests-macron.html.

52 Michael Shellenberger, "Number One In Poverty, California Isn't Our Most Progressive State – It's Our Most Racist One," *Forbes*, May 31, 2018, https://www.forbes.com/sites/michaelshellenberger/2018/05/31/number-one-in-poverty-california-isnt-our-most-progressive-state-its-our-most-racist-one/#6198645c-d9c3.

53 Mark Schneider, "Higher Education Pays: But a Lot More for Some Graduates Than for Others," American Institutes for Research, 2013, https://www.air.org/sites/default/files/Higher_Education_Pays_Sep_13.pdf

54 Camille Phillips, "San Antonio Poverty Rate Tops List Of Large Metro Areas," Texas Public Radio, Sept. 26, 2019, https://www.tpr.org/education/2019-09-26/san-antonio-poverty-rate-tops-list-of-large-metro-areas.

55 Wendell Cox, "Reducing Vehicle Miles Travelled Produces Meager Greenhous Gas Emissions Returns," *New Geography*, Aug. 6, 2009, https://www.newgeography.com/content/00950-reducing-vehicle-miles-traveled-produces-meager-greenhouse-gas-emission-reduction-retu.

56 Jennifer Hernandez and Joel Kotkin, "California Getting Its Own Way," Chapman University Center for Demographics and Policy, 2019, https://www.hklaw.com/-/media/files/insights/publications/2019/12/coureport.pdf?la=en.

57 Hank Adler, "A California Plan to Chase Away the Rich, Then Keep Stalking Them," *Wall Street Journal*, Dec. 18, 2020, https://www.wsj.com/articles/a-california-plan-to-chase-away-the-rich-then-keep-stalking-them-11608331448.

Chapter 2

1   "Housing markets" in this chapter refers to metropolitan areas.

2   Metropolitan areas over 1,000,000 population as of 2015.

3   Edward Glaeser and Joseph Gyourko (2019), "The Economic Implications of Housing Supply," *Journal of Economic Perspectives,* https://pubs.aeaweb.org/doi/pdf/10.1257/jep.32.1.3.

4   Gabriel Petek (February 2019), *The 2019-2020 Budget: Considerations for the Governor's Housing Plan,* https://lao.ca.gov/Publications/Report/3941.

5   The last pre-pandemic year.

6   *Demographia International Housing Affordability Survey: 2020.*

7   There has been considerable attention to the house price increases that have occurred around the country during the pandemic. These increases have been broad, and not materially altered the differences between California and the rest of the nation. From the first quarter of 2020 to the first quarter of 2021, National Association of Realtors data indicates that median house prices have risen 16.2%. The seven major markets of California have had a 17.0% average price increase over the same period of time.

8   National Association of Realtors, "Qualifying Income Based on Sales Price of Existing Single-Family Homes for Metropolitan Areas," Second Quarter 2019.

9   *Economic Report of the President and Annual Report of the Council of Economic Advisors* (ERP), 2020, https://www.govinfo.gov/content/pkg/ERP-2020/pdf/ERP-2020-chapter8.pdf.

10 ERP 2020.

11 Based on the cost of living adjusted median household income. See: Wendell Cox (May 2020), *URI Standard of Living Index*, Urban Reform Institute, https://secureservercdn.net/192.169.223.13/be6.064.myftpupload.com/wp-content/uploads/2020/05/URI-2020-Standard-of-Living-Index.pdf.

12 For example see John M. Quigley and Stephen Raphael (2005), "Regulation and the High Cost of Housing in California," https://escholarship.org/uc/item/90m9g90w, William A. Fischel (1995), *Regulatory Takings: Law, Economics, and Politics,* Harvard University Press, ERP (2020), Wendell Cox, "A Question of Values: Middle-Income Housing Affordability and Urban Containment Policy. Frontier Centre for Public Policy. https://fcpp.org/sites/default/files/documents/Cox%20-%20A%20Question%20of%20Values.pdf.

13 William A. Fischel (1995). *Regulatory Takings: Law, Economics, and Politics*. Harvard University Press.

14 Fischel (1995).

15 Also called "growth management."

16 Local General Government Units: US Metropolitan Areas over 1,000,000 Population: 2020 Metropolitan Area Definitions (Counties), http://www.demographia.com/db-msagovts2012.pdf. As currently defined, the San Francisco Bay Area has at least 82 municipalities, including 65 in the San Francisco metropolitan area and 17 in the San Jose metropolitan area. Los Angeles has 122 municipalities, Riverside-San Bernardino 52, Sacramento 19, San Diego 18 (government units based on the 2012 US Census of Governments).

17   Vacant land, especially on or beyond the urban fringe.

18   Tim Anaya (April 22, 2021), "CEQA strikes again in holding up major home-building project," *Right by the Bay*, Pacific Research Institute. https://www.pacificresearch.org/ceqa-strikes-again-in-holding-up-major-homebuilding-project/.

19   Bernard J. Frieden, *The Environmental Protection Hustle*, Cambridge, Mass.: MIT Press, 1979.

20   David E. Dowall (1984), *The Suburban Squeeze: Land Conversion and Regulation in the San Francisco Bay Area*, University of California Press.

21   National Impact Fee Survey: 2019, Impactfees.com, http://www.impactfees.com/publications%20pdf/2019survey.pdf.

22   For example, in 2016-7, city of Fremont impact fees were $19.1 million, nearly double that of the city of Los Angeles ($10.3 million), while the population of Los Angeles is more than 15 times that of Fremont.

23   See: "Improving Impact Fees in California: Rethinking the Nexus Study Requirement (2020)," Terner Center for Housing Innovation: UC Berkeley, https://ternercenter.berkeley.edu/blog/improving-impact-fees-in-california-rethinking-the-nexus-studies-requirements/.

24   "Residential Impact Fees in California (2019)," Terner Center for Housing Innovation: UC Berkeley, https://ternercenter.berkeley.edu/wp-content/uploads/pdfs/Residential_Impact_Fees_in_California_August_2019.pdf.

25   Through, for example Senate Bill 375 (2008).

26   Edge of the continuously developed urban area.

27   See William Alonso, *Location and Land Use: Toward a General Theory of Land Rent*, Harvard University Press, 1964. This concept assumes a mono-centric metropolitan area with a single dominating central business district. In recent decades, metropolitan areas around the world have become more polycentric, with peaks in land prices at the location of secondary centers ("edge cities") but generally below the values achieved in the central business district.

28   CEQA is not a land-use strategy, but is environmental regulation that has worked as an urban containment strategy.

29   Arthur C. Nelson and Casey J. Dawkins, "Urban Containment in the United States: History, Models and Techniques for Regional and Metropolitan Growth Management," American Planning Association Planning Advisory Service, https://www.researchgate.net/publication/288101674_Urban_containment_in_the_United_States_History_models_and_techniques_for_regional_and_metropolitan_growth_management (2004).

30   Arthur C. Nelson, Thomas W. Sanchez and Casey J. Dawkins (2004), "The Effect of Urban Containment and Mandatory Housing Elements on Racial Segregation in the United States," *Journal of Urban Affairs*. https://citeseerx.ist.psu.edu/viewdoc/download?doi=10.1.1.521.4467&rep=rep1&type=pdf.

31 Arthur C. Nelson and Casey J. Dawkins, "Urban Containment in the United States: History, Models and Techniques for Regional and Metropolitan Growth Management," American Planning Association Planning Advisory Service (2004), https://www.researchgate.net/publication/288101674_Urban_containment_in_the_United_States_History_models_and_techniques_for_regional_and_metropolitan_growth_management.

32 Figure is adapted from other works dealing urban growth boundaries. Other graphical representations of this relationship can be found in Gerrit Knaap and Arthur C. Nelson, "The Regulated Landscape: Lessons on State Land Use Planning from Oregon," Cambridge, Massachusetts: Lincoln Institute of Land Policy, 1992; William A. Fischel, "Zoning Rules! The Economics of Land-use Regulation," Lincoln Institute of Land Policy, 2015; Gerard Mildner, "Public Policy & Portland's Real Estate Market," *Quarterly and Urban Development Journal,* 4th Quarterly 2009: 1-16, and others. Under traditional land use regulation, where there is no urban containment boundary, Under "Traditional Regulation", the land price gradient would be smooth (the green line labeled "Before Urban Growth Boundary"). On the other hand, an abrupt increase occurs at the urban boundary in an environment with an urban containment boundary (the red line labeled "After Urban Growth Boundary").

33 Arthur C. Nelson and Casey J. Dawkins, "Urban Containment in the United States: History, Models and Techniques for Regional and Metropolitan Growth Management," American Planning Association Planning Advisory Service, https://www.researchgate.net/publication/288101674_Urban_containment_in_the_United_States_History_models_and_techniques_for_regional_and_metropolitan_growth_management (2004).

34 Nelson Casey J. Dawkins (2004).

35 Demographia (2021), "State Urban Density: 2000-2010," http://www.demographia.com/db-stateurbdensitych2000-2010.pdf.

36 Cox (May 2020).

37 Livable California (February 7, 2021), "Vancouver's Smartest Planner, Prof. Patrick Condon, Says Upzoning is a Costly Mistake," https://www.livable-california.org/vancouver-smartest-planner-prof-patrick-condon-calls-california-upzoning-a-costly-mistake-2-6-21/.

38 Derived from Census of Canada 1961 and 2016.

39 Livable California (February 7, 2021).

40 Patrick Condon (February 6, 2021), Presentation to Livable California, https://www.youtube.com/watch?v=24vf2c9AIwQ&t=8s.

41 *Demographia International Housing Affordability Survey,* and Canadian Housing and Mortgage Corporation (2020), "Rental Market Survey Tables," https://www.cmhc-schl.gc.ca/en/data-and-research/data-tables/rental-market-report-data-tables.

42 Derived from Census of Canada, 1971.

43 Authors review of median multiple data from US Census Bureau, *Demographia International Housing Affordability*, and Harvard University Joint Center for Housing Studies data.

44 *Demographia International Housing Affordability Survey.*

45 Derived from American Community Survey, 2018.

46 Derived from American Housing Survey 2011 and 2013.

47 Shlomo Angel, Patrick Lamson-Hall, Alejandro Blei, Sharad Shingade and Suman Kumar (2021), "Densify and Expand: A Global Analysis of Recent Urban Growth," *Sustainability.* https://www.mdpi.com/2071-1050/13/7/3835

48 Hall served as president of the Town and Country Planning Association of the United Kingdom.

49 Peter Geoffrey Hall, Ray Thomas, Harry Gracey and Roy Drewett (1973). *The Containment of Urban England: The Planning System: Objectives Operations, Impacts.* Vol. 2 Allen and Unwin [for] PEP, 1973.

50 Peter Geoffrey Hall et al (1973).

51 Calculated from data in Mariano Kulish, Anthony Richards and Christian Gillitzer, "Urban Structure and Housing Prices: Some Evidence from Australian Cities," Research Discussion Paper, Reserve Bank of Australia, September 2011. http://www.rba.gov.au/publications/rdp/2011/pdf/rdp2011-03.pdf.

52 Grimes, Arthur and Yun Liang (2008). "Spatial Determinants of Land Prices: Does Auckland's Metropolitan Urban Limit Have an Effect?" *Applied Spatial Analysis and Policy.* https://link.springer.com/article/10.1007/s12061-008-9010-8.

53 Gerard Mildner (2009), "Public Policy & Portland's Real Estate Market," *Quarterly and Urban Development Journal* (Fourth Quarter), www.pdx.edu/sites/www.pdx.edu.realestate/files/1Q10-4A-Mildner-UGB-1-31-10.pdf. https://web.archive.org/web/20150620083722/www.pdx.edu/sites/www.pdx.edu.realestate/files/1Q10-4A-Mildner-UGB-1-31-10.pdf.

54 Kate Barker, *Barker Review of Land Use Planning,* Norwich, England: Her Majesty's Stationary Office, 2006. Available online at https://www.gov.uk/government/uploads/system/uploads/attachment_data/file/228605/0118404857.pdf.

55 Benjamin Dachis (2018), *A Roadmap to Municipal Reform: Improving Life in Canadian Cities,* C.D. Howe Institute, https://www.cdhowe.org/sites/default/files/attachments/research_papers/mixed/Book_Road%20Map_Final_web.pdf.

56 *Demographia International Housing Affordability Survey.*

57 Land costs include all costs but construction.

58 All 92 major markets in *Demographia International Housing Affordability* rated severely unaffordable have urban containment. See: Wendell Cox (2021), *Demographia International Housing Affordability: 2021.* Urban Reform Institute and Frontier Centre for Public Policy,https://urbanreforminstitute.org/2021/02/demographia-international-housing-affordability-2021-edition/.

59 "Solly Angel Discusses the Complex Challenges of the Development and Expansion of Cities" (2021), *Marron Newsletter 3.3.21,* NYU Marron Institute of Urban Management, https://marroninstitute.nyu.edu/blog/marron-newsletter-3.3.21.

60 Gruen, Claude (2010), *New Urban Development: Looking Back to See Forward*, Rutgers University Press.

61   Calculated from 2017 US Census of Agriculture and 2010 US Census data.

62   John Fraser Hart (July 2001), "Half a Century of Cropland Change," *Geographical Review,* https://onlinelibrary.wiley.com/doi/abs/10.1111/j.1931-0846.2001.tb00239.x.

63   Inflation adjusted.

64   See Glaeser and Gyourko, above.

65   Derived from the US Census of Agriculture, 2017.

66   William Larson, Jessica Shui, Morris Davis, Stephan Oliner, "Working Paper 19-01: The Price of Residential Land for Counties, ZIP codes, and Census Tracts in the United States," Federal Housing Finance Agency www.fhfa.gov/PolicyProgramsResearch/Research/Pages/wp1901.aspx.

67   The London "greenbelt."

68   Wendell Cox (December 6, 2014), "Cities Better Off for the Great Suburbanization," *The New Geography.* http://www.newgeography.com/content/004794-cities-better-great-suburbanization.

69   Anthony Downs (1994), *New Visions for Metropolitan America*, Brookings Institution Press.

70   ERP, 2020.

71   Liana Fox, "The Supplemental Poverty Measure: 2019," United States Census Bureau, https://www.census.gov/library/publications/2020/demo/p60-272.html#~:text=The%20SPM%20rate%20for%202019,were%20initially%20published%20for%202009.

72   San Francisco Housing Authority, "Affordable Housing Online" (accessed May 26, 2021), https://affordablehousingonline.com/housing-authority/California/San-Francisco-Housing-Authority/CA001.

73   Cox (May 2021).

74   See: Hsieh, C., and E. Moretti. 2019. "Housing Constraints and Spatial Misallocation." *American Economic Journal: Macroeconomics.* And Glaeser, Edward, and Joseph Gyourko. 2018. "The Economic Implications of Housing Supply." *Journal of Economic Perspectives.*

75   Herkenhoff, K., L. Ohanian, and E. Prescott. 2018. "Tarnishing the Golden and Empire States: Land-Use Restrictions and the U.S. Economic Slowdown." *Journal of Monetary Economics.* https://www.nber.org/system/files/working_papers/w23790/w23790.pdf.

76   Calculated from US Census Bureau annual population estimates.

77   The Mojave Desert portion of Los Angeles County.

78   This concept was first proposed in Joel Kotkin, Marshall Toplansky, Wendell Cox, Mike Christienson, and Karla Lopez del Rio (2020), *Beyond Feudalism: A Policy to Restore California's Middle-Class,* Chapman University Center for Demographics and Policy, https://www.chapman.edu/communication/_files/beyond-feudalism-web-sm.pdf.

79   "In San Jose, Governor Newsom Signs Legislation to Fast-Track Key Housing, Economic Development Projects in California" May 20, 2021, Office of Governor Gavin Newsom, https://www.gov.ca.gov/2021/05/20/in-san-jose-governor-newsom-signs-legislation-to-fast-track-key-housing-economic-development-projects-in-california/.

CHAPTER 3

1   The number of homeless people as measured by the Department of Housing and Urban Development (HUD), https://www.hudexchange.info/resource/5948/2019-ahar-part-1-pit-estimates-of-homelessness-in-the-us/.

2   Janie Har, "Audit: California should track homeless spending, set policy, Associated Press, Feb. 11, 2021 https://apnews.com/article/california-coronavirus-pandemic-homelessness-dac338003e3f78986bc9369430cddd0b.

3   See: "Cost of Living" Federal Reserve Bank of St. Louis; https://research.stlouisfed.org/publications/cost-of-living/calculator, accessed March 11, 2021.

4   Sara Kimberlin, "California's Housing Affordability Crisis Hits Renters and Households With the Lowest Incomes the Hardest," California Budget & Policy Center, April 2019, https://calbudgetcenter.org/wp-content/uploads/2019/04/Report_California-Housing-Affordability-Crisis-Hits-Renters-and-Households-With-the-Lowest-Incomes-the-Hardest_04.2019.pdf.

5   The Council of Community and Economic Research maintains a Cost-of-Living Index that ranks regions based on the "cost of consumer goods and services, excluding taxes and non-consumer expenditures; see: "Annual 2020 Cost of Living Index Release," Council of Community and Economic Research, March 2021. The index measures the relative cost for more than "90,000 prices covering almost 60 different items," from "housing, utilities, grocery items, transportation, health care, and miscellaneous goods and services."

6   See: U.S. Census Income Tables: https://www.census.gov/topics/income-poverty/income.html, accessed March 12, 2021.

7   See for instance: Eli Saslow, "A 'virtual get-out-of-jail-free card': A new California law to reduce prison crowding keeps one addict out of jail, but not out of trouble," *Washington Post*, Oct. 10, 2015, https://www.washingtonpost.com/sf/national/2015/10/10/prop47/?utm_term=.37cab91d77db.

8   John Hirschauer, "Why Didn't the Supreme Court Take This Homelessness Case?" *National Review*, Jan. 8, 2020, https://www.nationalreview.com/2020/01/why-didnt-the-supreme-court-take-this-homelessness-case/.

9   Ramona Russell, "How Prop. 47 Fueled the Homeless Epidemic: Top law enforcement official says failed state policies are responsible for the drug addiction and mental illness crisis" *California Globe*, Feb. 24, 2020, https://californiaglobe.com/section-2/how-prop-47-fueled-the-homeless-epidemic/.

10 Mia Bird, Magnus Lofstrom, Brandon Martin, Steven Raphael, and Viet Nguyen, "The Impact of Proposition 47 on Crime and Recidivism," Public Policy Institute of California, June 2018, https://www.ppic.org/publication/the-impact-of-proposition-47-on-crime-and-recidivism/.

11 Edward Ring, "America's Homeless Industrial Complex – Causes & Solutions" California Policy Center, July 17, 2019, https://californiapolicycenter.org/americas-homeless-industrial-complex-causes-solutions/.

12 "Opening Doors: Federal Strategic Plan to End Homelessness," President Barack Obama, 2010.

13   Andy Helmer, "Homelessness requires a private sector solution," *The Tennessean*, November 15, 2017, https://www.tennessean.com/story/opinion/2017/11/15/homelessness-requires-private-sector-solution/865414001/.

14   Ibid.

15   Mindy Nakamura, "Addressing Homelessness Through the Private Sector," University of Tennessee, April 7, 2011, https://trace.tennessee.edu/cgi/viewcontent.cgi?referer=https://www.google.com/&httpsredir=1&article=2395&context=utk_chanhonoproj.

16   Ibid.

17   See: https://www.interventionca.org/, accessed March 16, 2021.

18   City of Santa Rosa, "Homeless Solutions," https://srcity.org/2485/Homelessness-Solutions.

19   Andrew Brown, "San Diego Homeless Tent Shelters To Stay Open Through June," KPBS, Sept. 18, 2018, https://www.kpbs.org/news/2018/sep/18/san-diego-homeless-tent-shelters-stay-open-june/.

CHAPTER 4

1 California Infrastructure Report Card 2021, https://infrastructurereport-card.org/state-item/california/.

2 Annual Highway Report 2020, https://reason.org/wp-content/up-loads/25th-annual-highway-report-state-by-state-summaries.pdf .

3 M. Nolan Gray, "How Californians Are Weaponizing Environmental Law," *Atlantic*, March 12, 2021 https://www.theatlantic.com/ideas/archive/2021/03/signature-environmental-law-hurts-housing/618264/.

4 See Edward Ring, "How Project Labor Agreements Elevate Costs to Taxpayers," California Policy Center, November 17, 2015, https://california-policycenter.org/how-project-labor-agreements-elevate-costs-to-taxpayers/ and Juan Rodriguez, "Project Labor Agreements (PLA) – Labor Agreement: Understanding Project Labor Agreements," *The Balance*, May 05, 2019, https://www.thebalancesmb.com/project-labor-agreements-pla-labor-agree-ment-844806.

5 Steven Greenhut, *Plunder: How Public Employee Unions are Raiding Treasuries, Controlling Our Lives and Bankrupting the Nation*, The Forum Press, 2009.

6 Bay Area Council Economic Institute, "Public-Private Partnerships in California," August 2018, http://www.bayareaeconomy.org/files/pdf/P3inCaliforni-aWeb.pdf.

7 Robert W. Poole Jr., *Rethinking America's Highways: A 21st- Century Vision for Better Infrastructure,* The University of Chicago Press, 2018.

CHAPTER 5

1   Editorial Board, "Drought crisis requires more long-term plans," *Orange County Register,* June 1, 2021, https://www.ocregister.com/2021/06/01/drought-crisis-requires-more-long-term-plans/.

2   Jeffrey Mount and Ellen Hanak, "Water Use in California," Public Policy Institute of California, May 2019, https://www.ppic.org/publication/water-use-in-california/.

3   U.S. Rep. Tom McClintock, R-Roseville, "The State of Water Supply Reliability," *Mymotherlode.com,* March 8, 2019, https://www.mymotherlode.com/news/local/595190/mcclintock-the-state-of-water-supply-reliability.html.

4   "Water Storage and Supply," California Department of Water Resources, accessed Feb. 28, 2020, https://water.ca.gov/What-We-Do/Water-Storage-And-Supply.

5   "California Water 101," Water Education Foundation, accessed Feb. 28, 2020, https://www.watereducation.org/photo-gallery/california-water-101.

6   Dan Walters, "Has Newsom Settled Water Wars?", *Davis Enterprise*, Feb. 9, 2020, https://www.davisenterprise.com/forum/dan-walters-has-newsom-settled-water-wars/.

7   Wallace Stegner, *The West as Living Space*, University of Michigan Press, 1987, https://www.goodreads.com/book/show/340535.The_American_West_as_Living_Space.

8   Goodwin J. Knight, governor, and Harvey O. Banks, director of water resources, "Bulletin No. 3 The California Water Plan," State of California, May 1957.

CHAPTER 6

1 See https://www.ed-data.org/state/CA.

2 Ibid.

3 Ibid.

4 Ibid.

5 "2019 Reading State Snapshot Report (California, Grade 8, Public Schools)," Institute for Education Sciences, National Center for Education Statistics, 2019, https://nces.ed.gov/nationsreportcard/subject/publications/stt2019/pdf/2020014CA8.pdf.

6 Ibid.

7 "2019 Math State Snapshot Report (California, Grade 8, Public Schools)," Institute for Education Sciences, National Center for Education Statistics, 2019, https://nces.ed.gov/nationsreportcard/subject/publications/stt2019/pdf/2020013CA8.pdf.

8 Ibid.

9 Libby Pier, Heather Hough, Michael Christian, Noah Bookman, Britt Wilkenfield, and Rick Miller, "COVID-19 and the Educational Equity Crisis," Policy Analysis for California Education (PACE), Jan. 25, 2021, available at https://edpolicyinca.org/newsroom/covid-19-and-educational-equity-crisis.

10 Ibid.

11 Ibid.

12 Ibid.

13 Ibid.

14 Ibid.

15 Ibid.

16 Richard Cano, "California pubic schools suffer record enrollment drop," *CalMatters,* Jan. 26, 2021, available at https://calmatters.org/education/2021/01/california-schools-record-enrollment-drop/.

17 Ibid.

18 See https://www.ccsa.org/charters-up-close/kids-first.

19 Ibid.

20 Ibid.

21 Ibid, p. 11.

22 "The Transition to Distance Learning Amid COVID-19," California Charter School Association, 2020, p. 6, https://f.hubspotusercontent30.net/hubfs/3049635/POM2020_FINAL.pdf.

23 "Competing rallies held over future of California charter schools," KCRA, May 22, 2019, https://www.kcra.com/article/competing-rallies-held-future-california-charter-schools/27562750.

24 Robin Lake, Ashley Jochim, Paul Hill, and Sivan Tuchman, "California Charter Schools: Costs, Benefits, and Impacts on School Districts," Center on Reinventing Public Education, University of Washington Bothell, May 2019, p. 1, https://www.crpe.org/sites/default/files/do_charter_schools_cause_fiscal_distress.pdf.

25 Ibid, p. 4.

26 Ibid, p. 5.

27 Todd Ziebarth, "Measuring Up to the Model: A Ranking of State Public Charter School Laws 2020," National Alliance for Public Charter Schools, January 2020, pp. 8-9, https://www.publiccharters.org/sites/default/files/documents/2020-01/2020_model_law_ranking_report-single-draft2%20%281%29.pdf.

28 Ibid, p. 5.

29 Ibid, p. 6.

30 According to the ranking of charter-school laws put out by the Center for Education Reform: "In a huge drop, California fell 16 spots. The Golden State plummeted because of adoption of a new law that allows districts enormous power over charter schools' fate and operations." See "State policies fail to keep up with the need for more and better education opportunities for students," Center for Education Reform, September 2020, available at https://edreform.com/2020/09/national-charter-school-law-rankings-and-scorecard-released/.

31 See https://leginfo.legislature.ca.gov/faces/billNavClient.xhtml?bill_id=201920200AB1505.

32 Ibid.

33 Ibid.

34 Ibid.

35 John Fensterwald, "Governor, lawmakers agree on new controls on California charter schools," EdSource, Aug. 29, 2019, https://edsource.org/2019/governor-lawmakers-agree-on-new-controls-on-california-charter-schools/616877.

36 Louis Freedberg and Michael Burke, "Impact of teacher activism in California being felt in multiple but less visible ways, leaders say," EdSource, Jan. 24, 2020, https://edsource.org/2020/impact-of-teacher-activism-in-california-being-felt-in-multiple-but-less-visible-ways-education-leaders-say/622878.

37 See https://leginfo.legislature.ca.gov/faces/billTextClient.xhtml?bill_id=201920200SB820.

38 See Serrano v. Priest, 557 P. 2d 929 – Cal: Supreme Court 1976, available at https://scholar.google.com/scholar_case?case=13633818682294589185&hl=en&as_sdt=2006 and see California Code, Education Code – EDC Section 42238.02, available at https://codes.findlaw.com/ca/education-code/edc-sect-42238-02.html.

39 See Amy Falk, et al., "COViD-19 Transmission in 17 K-12 Schools—Wood County, Wisconsin, August 31-November 29, 2020," Morbidity and Mortality Weekly Report, Centers for Disease Control and Prevention, January 29, 2021, available at https://www.cdc.gov/mmwr/volumes/70/wr/mm7004e3.htm.

40 Ibid.

41 See https://www.publiccharters.org/our-work/charter-law-database.

42 See https://www.wvlegislature.gov/Bill_Text_HTML/2021_SESSIONS/RS/bills/HB2013%20SUB%20ENR.pdf.

43   Corey DeAngelis, "Funding Students Instead of Institutions," Georgia
      Public Policy Foundation, Jan. 27, 2021, https://www.georgiapolicy.
      org/2021/01/funding-students-instead-of-institutions/.

44   "Study Shows Long-Term Benefits in Georgia Education Scholarship Ac-
      counts," Georgia Public Policy Foundation, Jan. 27, 2021, https://www.
      georgiapolicy.org/2021/01/study-shows-long-term-benefits-in-georgia-ed-
      ucation-scholarship-accounts/.

CHAPTER 7

1   Philip Reese, "Homicides Surge in California as COVID Shutters Schools, Youth Programs," *US News and World Report*, May 17, 2021, https://www.usnews.com/news/best-states/articles/2021-05-17/homicides-surge-in-california-amid-covid-shutdowns-of-schools-youth-programs.

2   Ibid.

3   Magnus Lofstrom and Brandon Martin, "California's Major Cities See Increases in Homicides and Car Thefts," Public Policy Institute of California, April 27, 2021, https://www.ppic.org/blog/californias-major-cities-see-increases-in-homicides-and-car-thefts/.

4   Charles Wright, "Violent crime in London falling overall, says Met deputy commissioner," *On London*, Jan 11., 2020, https://www.onlondon.co.uk/violent-crime-in-london-falling-overall-says-met-deputy-commissioner/

5   Macro Trends: https://www.macrotrends.net/countries/ITA/italy/murder-homicide-rate.

6   "Crime in Japan Drops to Lowest Post-War Level, 2020 Data Show," *VOA News*, Feb. 4, 2021, https://www.voanews.com/east-asia-pacific/crime-japan-drops-lowest-post-war-level-2020-data-show.

7   "April homicides down 3.5%; first 4 months down 4% compared to last year," *Mexico Daily News*, May 22, 2021, https://mexiconewsdaily.com/news/april-homicides-decline-3-5/.

8   Evan Sernoffsky, "SF supervisor leads anti-police-union 'F- the POA' chant at DA election party," *San Francisco Chronicle*, Nov. 6, 2019, https://www.sfchronicle.com/crime/article/SF-supervisor-leads-anti-police-union-F-the-14814220.php.

9   Leslie Ridgeway, USC Gould School of Law, "Philadelphia DA Larry Krasner discusses criminal justice in action with Prof. Jody Armour," Dec. 13, 2019, https://gould.usc.edu/about/news/?id=4642.

10 California Department of Corrections and Rehabilitation: https://www.cdcr.ca.gov/budget/, accessed June 20, 2021.

11 California Innocence Project recidivism data: https://californiainnocenceproject.org/issues-we-face/recidivism-rates/#:~:text=Recidivism%20rates%20by%20state%20vary,system%20return%20within%20three%20years, accessed June 20, 2021.

12 U.S. Department of Justice, Bureau of Justice Statistics, "Reentry Trends in the United States," https://www.prisonpolicy.org/scans/bjs/reentry.pdf, accessed June 20, 2021.

13 Trevor Freeman, "Drug Abuse in the States: Incarceration," Trevor Freeman's blog, Aug. 28, 2017, https://knowledgecenter.csg.org/kc/content/drug-abuse-states-incarceration.

14 Jolie McCullough, "Texas prisons stopped in-person visits and limited mail. Drugs got in anyway," *Texas Tribune*, March 29, 2021, https://www.texastribune.org/2021/03/29/texas-prisons-drugs/.

15   American Psychological Association data: https://www.apa.org/mon-
      itor/2014/10/incarceration#:~:text=While%20at%20least%20half%20
      of,or%20schizophrenia%2C%20the%20report%20finds.

16   King County, WA, explanation of LEAD program: https://kingcounty.gov/
      depts/community-human-services/mental-health-substance-abuse/diver-
      sion-reentry-services/lead.aspx.

17   "California Department of Corrections and Rehabilitation: Several Poor Ad-
      ministrative Practices Have Hindered Reductions in Recidivism and Denied
      Inmates Access to In-Prison Rehabilitation Programs," California State Audi-
      tor report on prison recidivism, January 2019, https://www.auditor.ca.gov/
      pdfs/reports/2018-113.pdf.

18   American Psychological Association, 2000, https://www.apa.org/news/
      press/releases/2000/08/faith.

19   The National Center on Addiction and Substance Abuse (CASA) at Co-
      lumbia University, 2003, https://www.ncbi.nlm.nih.gov/pmc/articles/
      PMC1526775/#R131.

20   "The Impact of Hawaii's HOPE Program on Drug Use, Crime and Re-
      cidivism," Pew Charitable Trusts, https://www.pewtrusts.org/en/re-
      search-and-analysis/reports/0001/01/01/the-impact-of-hawaiis-hope-pro-
      gram-on-drug-use-crime-and-recidivism.

21   State of California, Rehabilitation Strike Team Report, 2007, https://crob.
      ca.gov/wp-content/uploads/2019/08/C-ROB-Biannual-Report-March-15-2009.
      pdf.

22   Robert Salonga, "A decade after emerging from captivity in the Bay Area,
      Jaycee Dugard reflects on the life she lost, and the one she's gained," *Denver
      Post*, Aug. 26, 2019, https://www.denverpost.com/2019/08/26/jaycee-du-
      gard-kidnapping-story-decade-later/.

23   Michael Rothfeld, "State prison watchdog strongly criticizes procedures in
      Jaycee Dugard case," *Los Angeles Times*, Nov. 5, 2009, https://www.latimes.
      com/archives/la-xpm-2009-nov-05-me-jaycee-dugard5-story.html.

24   Maurice Chammah, "Rape in the American Prison," *The Atlantic*, Feb. 25,
      2015, https://www.theatlantic.com/politics/archive/2015/02/rape-in-the-
      american-prison/385550/.

25   Alysia Santo, "Prison Rape Allegations Are on the Rise," The Marshall Proj-
      ect, July 25, 2018, https://www.themarshallproject.org/2018/07/25/prison-
      rape-allegations-are-on-the-rise.

CHAPTER 8

1   2021-22 Governor's Budget Summary, Appendix 13, http://www.ebudget.ca.gov/2021-22/pdf/BudgetSummary/FullBudgetSummary.pdf.

2   David Crane, Stanford Institute for Economic Policy Research, Presentation to SIEPR Associates, Aug. 18, 2020, https://www.youtube.com/watch?v=AwnRN4tdo5M&t=1s.

3   Legislative Analyst's Office, "The 2021-22 Budget: California's Fiscal Outlook," https://lao.ca.gov/Budget?year=2021&subjectArea=outlook.

4   2021-22 Governor's Budget Summary, p. 243 (see link above).

5   Legislative Analyst's Office, "The 2021-22 Budget: Analysis of the Major University Proposals," Feb. 1, 2021, https://lao.ca.gov/Publications/Report/4336.

6   California Tax Facts, California Taxpayers Foundation, April 2021, p. 16, https://www.caltax.org/foundation/reports/2021-Tax-Facts.pdf.

7   Legislative Analyst's Office, "The 2021-22 Budget: The Governor's Proposition 2 Proposals," April 26, 2021, https://lao.ca.gov/Publications/Report/4418.

8   2021-22 Governor's Budget Summary, p. 240 (see link above).

9   Organisation for Economic Co-operation and Development, "Effective Tax Rates," 2019, https://stats.oecd.org/Index.aspx?DataSetCode=CTS_ETR.

10   George Skelton, "Capitol Journal: A smart California tax bill points the way to needed reform," *Los Angeles Times,* Dec. 17, 2014, https://www.latimes.com/local/politics/la-me-cap-hertzberg-20141218-column.html.

11   Senate and Assembly Bill Analyses of Senate Bill 400 of 1999, https://leginfo.legislature.ca.gov/faces/billAnalysisClient.xhtml?bill_id=199920000SB400.

12   "CalPERS Comprehensive Annual Financial Report," Fiscal Year Ended June 30, 2020, p. 126, https://www.calpers.ca.gov/docs/forms-publications/cafr-2020.pdf.

13   "CalPERS Reports Preliminary 4.7% Investment Return for Fiscal Year 2019-20," California Public Employees' Retirement System, July 15, 2020 https://www.calpers.ca.gov/page/newsroom/calpers-news/2020/calpers-preliminary-investment-return-2019-20.

14   California State Controller's Office, "Agent Multiple-Employer Defined Benefit Other Postemployment Benefits (OPEB) Plans Schedule of OPEB Pay-As-You-Go Contributions, Schedule of OPEB Prefunding Contributions, Schedule of Retiree Headcount, and Schedule of OPEB Amounts for the Fiscal Year Ended June 30, 2019," Note 7, p. 26 https://www.sco.ca.gov/Files-ARD/CAFR/OPEBauc805webposting2020.pdf.

15   Ibid, Note 8.

16   "UC Borrows $2.7 billion to fund pension debt," UCnet, July 28, 2014 https://newsroom.ucla.edu/dept/faculty/uc-borrows-2-7-billion-to-fund-pension-debt.

17   "Comprehensive Annual Financial Report of the California State Teachers
      Retirement System for the Fiscal Year Ended June 30, 2020," California State
      Teachers' Retirement System, p. 27, https://www.calstrs.com/sites/main/
      files/file-attachments/cafr2020.pdf?1608578677.

18   Lee Ohanian, 2020 UC Berkeley Baxter Liberty Lecture, "The Tarnishing
      of the Golden State: How Poorly Designed Policies Killed the California
      Dream," Dec. 8, 2020, https://economics.ucla.edu/2020/12/08/ohanian_
      ucb_baxterliberty.

19   California State Auditor, Reports 2015-608 and 2017-601, https://www.
      auditor.ca.gov/pdfs/reports/2015-608.pdf https://www.auditor.ca.gov/pdfs/
      reports/2015-608.pdf.

20   Legislative Analyst's Office, "The 2014-15 Budget: Capital Outlay Support
      Program," May 14, 2014, https://lao.ca.gov/reports/2014/budget/capital-out-
      lay/capital-outlay-support-program-051414.aspx.

21   Assembly members Jay Obernolte and Sharon Quirk-Silva, "California As-
      sembly's New Rules have led to Legislative Censorship, *CalMatters*, May 29,
      2019, https://www.desertsun.com/story/opinion/columnists/2019/05/29/
      california-assembly-new-rules-have-brought-legislative-censorship-calmat-
      ters-commentary/1275335001/#.

22   *Cal Fire Local 2881 v. California Public Employees' Retirement System*,
      March 4, 2019 (S239958, ___ Cal.4th___) https://law.justia.com/cases/cali-
      fornia/supreme-court/2019/s239958.html.

23   Mary Williams Walsh, Rhode Island Averts Pension Disaster Without
      Raising Taxes, *New York Times*, Sept. 26, 2015, https://www.nytimes.
      com/2015/09/26/business/dealbook/rhode-island-averts-pension-disas-
      ter-without-raising-taxes.html.

24   Assembly Constitutional Amendment 27 of 2006, authored by Assembly
      member Kevin McCarthy.

25   Ballot arguments in support of Proposition 1-A, "California General Election
      Voter Guide," Nov. 4, 2008, https://repository.uchastings.edu/cgi/viewcon-
      tent.cgi?article=2265&context=ca_ballot_props.

26   See for example, Legislative Analyst's Office, "The 2017-18 Budget: Gover-
      nor's Gann Limit Proposal," March 2, 2017, and; Legislative Analyst's Of-
      fice, "The 2018-19 Budget: Governor's Gann Limit Estimates," April 6, 2018
      https://lao.ca.gov/Publications/Report/3596 and https://lao.ca.gov/Publica-
      tions/Report/3800.

27   Legislative Analyst's Office, "The State Appropriations Limit," April 23, 2021,
      https://lao.ca.gov/reports/2021/4416/SAL-042121.pdf .

CHAPTER 9

1   Senate Bill No. X1 2. (2011-2012 session).

2   Senate Bill No. 350 (2015-2016 session).

3   Senate Bill No. 100 (2017-2018 session).

4   Legislative Analyst's Office, "The 2020-2021 Budget: Governor's Wildfire-Related Proposals," Feb. 21, 2020, p. 5.

5   Steven Greenhut, *Winning the Water Wars*, (Pacific Research Institute: 2020), p. 104.

6   Legislative Analyst's Office, "The 2020-21 Budget: Governor's Wildfire-Related Proposals," Feb. 21, 2020, p. 5.

7   Jim Carlton, "Lightning, Winds and Heat Set Table for Wildfires in the West," *Wall Street Journal,* Sept. 11, 2020, p. A6.

8   Ibid.

9   Ibid.

10 Ibid.

11 Of course, a percentage of the carbon released in the fires will be reabsorbed as the forest regrows over time.

12 Legislative Analyst's Office, "The 2021-22 Budget: Wildfire Resilience Package," Feb. 5, 2021, p. 4.

13 Dale Kasler and Nicole Blanchard, "Burning California to save it: Why one solution to raging wildfires can't gain traction," *Sacramento Bee*, Feb. 25, 2021, https://www.sacbee.com/news/california/fires/article249345695.html.

14 Legislative Analyst's Office, "The 2021-22 Budget: Cap-and-Trade Expenditure Plan," Feb. 10, 2021, p. 3.

15 Ibid. In deriving the $200 million figure, the Legislative Analyst added $75 million in statutory allocations to discretionary spending of $125 million for CAL FIRE.

16 Legislative Analyst's Office, "The 2020-21 Budget: Governor's Wildfire-Related Proposals," p. 9; Gary Ferguson, *Land on Fire* (Timber Press 2017), p. 158.

17 Kasler and Blanchard, "Burning California to save it: Why one solution to raging wildfires can't gain traction," *Sacramento Bee*, Feb. 25, 2021, https://www.sacbee.com/news/california/fires/article249345695.html.

18 Gary Ferguson, *Land on Fire* (Timber Press 2017), p. 158, https://www.amazon.com/Land-Fire-Reality-Wildfire-West/dp/1604697008.

19 Ibid.

20 James MacDonald, "Does Forest Thinning Work?" *JSTOR Daily*, Oct. 10, 2019, citing Sharon M. Hood, Stephen Baker and Anna Sala, "Fortifying the forest: thinning and burning increase resistance to a bark beetle outbreak and promote forest resilience," in *Ecological Applications*, vol. 26, no. 7, 2016, https://daily.jstor.org/does-forest-thinning-work/.

21 Gary Ferguson, *Land on Fire*, p. 165.

22   Dale Kasler and Nicole Blanchard, "Burning California to save it: Why one solution to raging wildfires can't gain traction," *Sacramento Bee*, Feb. 25, 2021, https://www.sacbee.com/news/california/fires/article249345695.html.

23   Governor's Office, "California's Wildfire and Forest Resilience Action Plan," January 2021, p. 18.

24   Dale Kasler and Nicole Blanchard, "Burning California to save it: Why one solution to raging wildfires can't gain traction," *Sacramento Bee*, Feb. 25, 2021, https://www.sacbee.com/news/california/fires/article249345695.html.

25   Ibid.

26   CAL FIRE, California Natural Resources Agency, and California Environmental Protection Agency, "California Forest Carbon Plan: Managing our Forest Landscapes in a Changing Climate," May 2018, p. 1 (hereinafter, CAL FIRE et al., California Forest Carbon Plan"), https://resources.ca.gov/CNRALegacy-Files/wp-content/uploads/2018/05/California-Forest-Carbon-Plan-Final-Draft-for-Public-Release-May-2018.pdf.

27   CAL FIRE et al., "California Forest Carbon Plan," p. 1, https://resources.ca.gov/CNRALegacyFiles/wp-content/uploads/2018/05/California-Forest-Carbon-Plan-Final-Draft-for-Public-Release-May-2018.pdf.

28   Gary Ferguson, *Land on Fire*, p. 165; CAL FIRE et al., "California Forest Carbon Plan," p. 1; see also Ferguson, *supra*, p. 1.

29   Mac Taylor, Legislative Analyst's Office, "Improving California's Forest and Watershed Management," April 2018, p. 5, https://lao.ca.gov/Publications/Report/3798.

30   Ibid., pp. 4-5; CAL FIRE et al., "California Forest Carbon Plan," p. 138.

31   Governor's Office Press Release, "California Certifies Statewide Programmatic Environmental Impact Review to Protect Californians from Catastrophic Wildfires," Dec. 31, 2019.

32   Office of Senate Floor Analyses, Analysis of Senate Bill No. 85, pp. 1, 3.

33   Ibid.

34   Governor's May Revision 2021-2022, p. 123.

35   Governor's Office, "California's Wildfire and Forest Resilience Action Plan," January 2021, p. 18, https://www.fire.ca.gov/media/ps4p2vck/californiawild-fireandforestresilienceactionplan.pdf.

36   Governor's May Revision 2021-2022, p. 123. The $608 million figure excludes an additional $100 million proposed for "defensible space inspectors, land use planning and outreach, "science-based management," "workforce training," and the "climate catalyst fund & market strategy," since these do not cover the costs of thinning forests or creating fire breaks.

37   Governor's May Revision 2021-2022, pp. 123, 125, 126-128.

38   CAL FIRE et al., "California Forest Carbon Plan," p. 56.

39   Dale Kasler and Nicole Blanchard, "Burning California to save it: Why one solution to raging wildfires can't gain traction," *Sacramento Bee*, Feb. 25, 2021, https://www.sacbee.com/news/california/fires/article249345695.html.

40   Ibid.

41   CAL FIRE et al., "California Forest Carbon Plan," May 2018, p. 56.

42 Public Resources Code section 4527.

43 CAL FIRE et al., "California Forest Carbon Plan," p. 138.

44 Ibid.

45 Ibid.

46 Jim Carlton, "Plans for Fire Protection Hit Red Tape in California," *Wall Street Journal*, Sept. 17, 2020, https://www.wsj.com/articles/a-california-towns-fire-protection-plans-hit-red-tape-then-it-burned-to-the-ground-11600335002.

47 California Government Code section 8558.

48 California Government Code section 8571.

49 CAL FIRE et al., "California Forest Carbon Plan," p. 2.

50 Governor's Forest Management Task Force, "California's Wildfire and Forest Resilience Action Plan," January 2021, pp. 36-37, https://www.fire.ca.gov/media/ps4p2vck/californiawildfireandforestresilienceactionplan.pdf.

51 Kirk Siegler, "Washington State Is Thinning Out Forests to Reduce Wildfire Risk," National Public Radio, Oct. 23, 2019, https://www.npr.org/2019/10/23/772775789/washington-state-is-thinning-out-forests-to-reduce-wildfire-risk#:~:text=Transcript-,The%20state%20of%20Washington%20is%20moving%20to%20aggressively%20thin%20forests,AILSA%20CHANG%2C%20HOST%3A&text=As%20the%20threat%20of%20wildfires,parts%20of%20the%20rural%20Northwest.

52 Governor's May Revision 2021-2022, p. 123.

53 Gary Ferguson, *Land on Fire* (Timber Press 2017), p. 170.

54 Legislative Analyst's Office, "The 2021-2022 Budget: Wildfire Resilience Package," Feb. 5, 2021, p. 11.

55 Gary Ferguson, *Land on Fire*, p. 168.

56 Katherine Blunt and Russell Gold, "PG&E Knew for Years Its Lines Could Spark Wildfires, and Didn't Fix Them," *Wall Street Journal*, July 10, 2019, https://www.wsj.com/articles/pg-e-knew-for-years-its-lines-could-spark-wildfires-and-didnt-fix-them-11562768885.

57 Ibid.

58 Legislative Analyst's Office, "The 2020-21 Budget: Governor's Wildfire-Related Proposals," Feb. 21, 2020, p. 5, https://lao.ca.gov/Publications/Report/4172#:~:text=Governor's%202020%E2%80%9121%20Budget%20Includes,million%20for%20CalFire%2C%20%2476.

59 Governor's Forest Management Task Force, "California's Wildfire and Forest Resilience Action Plan," p. 31, https://www.fire.ca.gov/media/ps4p2vck/californiawildfireandforestresilienceactionplan.pdf.

60 Ibid.

61 Quoted in Gary Ferguson, *Land on Fire*, p. 155.

62 Dale Kasler and Daniel Hunt, "PG&E Equipment Caused Deadly Zogg Fire in Shasta County," *Sacramento Bee,* March 22, 2021, https://www.sacbee.com/news/california/fires/article250134899.html.

CHAPTER 10

1   Alex Rogers, "Senate narrowly confirms Xavier Becerra as Health and Human Services secretary," CNN, March 18, 2021, https://www.cnn.com/2021/03/18/politics/xavier-becerra-confirmation-vote/index.html.

2   California Attorney General Press Release, "Attorney General Becerra Leads Coalition of 20 States and the District of Columbia Defending the ACA in U.S. Supreme Court, May 6,2020, https://oag.ca.gov/news/press-releases/attorney-general-becerra-leads-coalition-20-states-and-district-columbia; MaryBeth Muscumeci, "Explaining *California v. Texas:* A Guide to the Case Challenging the ACA," Kaiser Family Foundation, Sept. 1, 2020, https://www.kff.org/health-reform/issue-brief/explaining-california-v-texas-a-guide-to-the-case-challenging-the-aca/.

3   Victoria Knight, "Becerra Has Long Backed Single-Payer. That Doesn't Mean It Will Happen if He's HHS Secretary, KNN, March 1, 2021, https://khn.org/news/article/fact-check-xavier-becerra-opposition-ads-single-payer-insurance-health-care-coverage/.

4   Sarah Kliff, "Becerra Supports 'Medicare for All,' and Could Help States Get There," *New York Times*, Dec. 10, 2020, https://www.nytimes.com/2020/12/10/upshot/becerra-medicare-for-all-waivers-hhs.html.

5   California Department of Health Care Services, "Medi-Cal Enrollment," https://www.dhcs.ca.gov/dataandstats/Pages/Medi-Cal-Eligibility-Statistics.aspx, accessed June 20, 2021.

6   Legislative Analyst's Office, "Analysis of the Medi-Cal Budget," Feb. 16, 2021, https://lao.ca.gov/Publications/Report/4373.

7   Harriet Blair Rowan, "Medi-Cal's Very Big Decade," KNN, Jan. 17, 2020, https://khn.org/news/medi-cals-very-big-decade/.

8   California Department of Health Care Services, "Statistical Briefs," https://www.dhcs.ca.gov/dataandstats/statistics/Pages/RASD_Statistical_Briefs.aspx#:~:text=California's%20government%20collects%20vast%20amounts,the%20nation's%20largest%20Medicaid%20program, accessed June 20, 2021.

9   Vanessa Romo, "California's Budget Proposal Would Expand Health Care To Some Undocumented Immigrants," National Public Radio, June 10, 2019, https://www.npr.org/2019/06/10/731311422/californias-budget-proposal-would-expand-health-care-to-some-undocumented-immigr.

10   Angela Hart, "California lawmakers to Gov, Newsom: Give all immigrants health coverage," *Kaiser Health News*, Dec. 10, 2020, https://medcitynews.com/2020/12/california-lawmakers-to-gov-newsom-give-all-immigrants-health-coverage/.

11   Sammy Caiola, "California To Provide Health Insurance For Undocumented Residents Over 50 Following Toll Of COVID-19," Capital Public Radio, July 1, 2021, https://www.capradio.org/articles/2021/07/01/california-to-provide-health-insurance-for-undocumented-residents-over-50-following-toll-of-covid-19/.

12   Kim Bojorquez, "Is California ready to open health care to undocu-
      mented adults? Latino leaders say yes," *Sacramento Bee*, April 9, 2021,
      https://www.sacbee.com/news/politics-government/capitol-alert/arti-
      cle250500984.html.

13   Janet Coffman and Margaret Fix, "Physician Participation in Medi-Cal: Is
      Supply Meeting Demand?" California Health Care Foundation, June 28,
      2017, https://www.chcf.org/publication/physician-participation-in-me-
      di-cal-is-supply-meeting-demand/.

14   California Franchise Tax Board information: https://www.ftb.ca.gov/about-
      ftb/newsroom/health-care-mandate/personal.html, accessed June 20, 2021.

15   Anna Porretta, "What You Need to Know About the Changes to California
      Health Insurance," eHealth, Nov. 23, 2020, https://www.ehealthinsurance.
      com/resources/individual-and-family/what-you-need-to-know-about-the-
      changes-to-california-health-insurance.

16   Carmin Chappell, "Trump administration makes it easier to avoid
      Obamacare tax penalty," CNBC, Sept. 12, 2018, https://www.cnbc.
      com/2018/09/12/cms-launches-new-process-to-claim-individual-man-
      date-penalty-exemption.html.

17   California Franchise Tax Board estimator: https://www.ftb.ca.gov/about-
      ftb/newsroom/tax-news/january-2020/california-individual-healthcare-man-
      date-penalty-estimator.html, accessed June 20, 2021.

18   "State Health Facts," Kaiser Family Foundation: https://www.kff.org/
      health-reform/state-indicator/marketplace-average-benchmark-premi-
      ums/?currentTimeframe=0&selectedDistributions=2021&sortMod-
      el=%7B%22colId%22:%22Location%22,%22sort%22:%22asc%22%7D,
      accessed June 20, 2021.

19   Margaret Beck, "You may pay less in 2020: Changes coming to Covered Cal-
      ifornia," *Redding Record Searchlight*, Sept. 27, 2019, https://www.redding.
      com/story/life/2019/09/27/you-may-pay-less-2020-changes-coming-covered-
      california/2440802001/.

20   John Myers, "California Gov. Gavin Newsom has signed his first budget.
      Here's where the $215 billion will go," *Los Angeles Times*, June 27, 2019,
      https://www.latimes.com/politics/la-pol-ca-california-government-spend-
      ing-budget-20190627-htmlstory.html.

21   Dylan Scott, "Exclusive: Nearly 7 million uninsured Americans qualify
      for free health insurance," *Vox*, April 1, 2021, https://www.vox.com/
      policy-and-politics/22360870/american-rescue-plan-act-premium-tax-cred-
      it-health-insurance.

22   Nicole Kaeding and Kari Jahnsen, "California Single-payer: A Dream for
      Expanded Coverage, a Nightmare to Fund," Tax Foundation, June 6, 2017,
      https://taxfoundation.org/california-single-payer-nightmare-to-fund/.

23   Dylan Scott, "California's single-payer plan costs $400 billion – twice
      the state's entire budget," *Vox*, May 22, 2017, https://www.vox.com/poli-
      cy-and-politics/2017/5/22/15676782/california-single-payer-health-care-esti-
      mate.

24   Nicole Kaeding and Kari Jahnsen, "California Single-payer: A Dream for
      Expanded Coverage, a Nightmare to Fund," Tax Foundation, June 6, 2017,

https://taxfoundation.org/california-single-payer-nightmare-to-fund/.

25 Clio Chang, "What Killed Single-Payer In California?" *New Republic*, June 30, 2017, https://newrepublic.com/article/143650/killed-single-payer-california.

26 Office of Gov. Gavin Newsom, "Governor Newsom Announces Healthy California for All Commission," Dec. 18, 2019, https://www.gov.ca.gov/2019/12/18/governor-newsom-announces-healthy-california-for-all-commission/.

27 Ibid.

28 Assembly Bill 1400: https://leginfo.legislature.ca.gov/faces/billNavClient.xhtml?bill_id=202120220AB1400.

29 Angela Hart and Rachel Bluth, "New Single-Payer Bill Intensifies Newsom's Political Peril," KHN, Feb. 19, 2021, https://khn.org/news/article/new-single-payer-bill-intensifies-newsoms-political-peril/.

30 Tweet, Emily Hoeven, https://twitter.com/emily_hoeven/status/1385033679739637760.

31 Eric Escalante, "Here's why another 650,000 people left California last year," ABC 10, Nov. 17, 2020, https://www.abc10.com/article/news/local/california/653000-people-leave-california/103-f3c88956-791a-43ca-bc8f-bcbaa76cf790.

32 Shelby Bracho, "People are leaving California at record rates," Fox 26 News, Feb. 4, 2021, https://kmph.com/news/local/people-are-leaving-california-at-record-rates#:~:text=FRESNO%2C%20Calif.,growth%20hit%20a%20record%20low.

33 U.S. Bureau of Labor Statistics, "Local Unemployment Statistics," https://www.bls.gov/web/laus/laumstrk.htm, accessed June 20, 2021.

34 Senate Bill 910: https://leginfo.legislature.ca.gov/faces/billTextClient.xhtml?bill_id=201720180SB910.

35 Brian Blase, "Individual Health Insurance Markets Improving in States that Fully Permit Short-Term Plans, Galen Institute, February 2021, https://galen.org/assets/Individual-Health-Insurance-Markets-Improving-in-States-that-Fully-Permit-Short-Term-Plans.pdf.

36 Sydney Garrow, "Short-Term Health Plans Cost 224 Percent Less than Obamacare Plans Per Month," eHealth, Nov. 7, 2019, https://www.ehealthinsurance.com/resources/individual-and-family/short-term-health-plans-cost-80-percent-less-obamacare-plans-per-month.

37 Chris Pope, "Renewable Term Health Insurance," Manhattan Institute, May 2019, https://media4.manhattan-institute.org/sites/default/files/R-0519-CP.pdf?mod=article_inline.

38 https://www.urban.org/research/publication/updated-potential-impact-short-term-limited-duration-policies-insurance-coverage-premiums-and-federal-spending.

39 Brian Blase, "Individual Health Insurance Markets Improving in States that Fully Permit Short-Term Plans, Galen Institute, February 2021, https://galen.org/assets/Individual-Health-Insurance-Markets-Improving-in-States-that-Fully-Permit-Short-Term-Plans.pdf.

40 "California Governor: Association Health Plans Are No More," Emplicity, March 4, 2020, https://emplicity.com/california-association-health-plans/.

41 Ibid.

42 Ibid.

43 Matthew D. Mitchell, Anne Philpott, Jessica McBirney, "CON Laws in 2020," Mercatus Center, Feb. 19 2021, https://www.mercatus.org/publications/healthcare/con-laws-2020-about-update#:~:text=Certificate%2Dof%2D-need%20(CON,undermine%20the%20quality%20of%20care.

44 Arianna Wilkerson, "States Do Not Need Certificate of Need Laws," Heartland Institute, April 26, 2019, https://www.heartland.org/publications-resources/publications/the-leaflet-states-do-not-need-certificate-of-need-laws.

45 Cheryl Sarfaty, "What it will mean for health care when California's nurse practitioners get more freedom under new law," *North Bay Business Journal*, Dec. 7, 2020, https://www.northbaybusinessjournal.com/article/industrynews/what-it-will-mean-for-health-care-when-californias-nurse-practitioners-get/.

46 American Association of Nurse Practitioners Fact Sheet: https://www.aanp.org/about/all-about-nps/np-fact-sheet#:~:text=There%20are%20more%20than%20290%2C000,NPs)%20licensed%20in%20the%20U.S.&text=More%20than%2030%2C000%20new%20NPs,academic%20programs%20in%202018%E2%80%932019.&text=89.7%25%20of%20NPs%20are%20certified,all%20NPs%20deliver%20primary%20care, accessed June 20, 2021.

47 American Association of Nurse Practitioners Fact Sheet: https://www.aanp.org/student-resources/planning-your-np-education, accessed June 20, 2021.

48 American Association of Nurse Practitioners Fact Sheet: https://www.aanp.org/about/all-about-nps/np-fact-sheet#:~:text=There%20are%20more%20than%20290%2C000,NPs)%20licensed%20in%20the%20U.S.&text=More%20than%2030%2C000%20new%20NPs,academic%20programs%20in%202018%E2%80%932019.&text=89.7%25%20of%20NPs%20are%20certified,all%20NPs%20deliver%20primary%20care, accessed June 20,2021.

49 American Medical Association, "Physician assistant scope of practice," https://www.ama-assn.org/sites/ama-assn.org/files/corp/media-browser/public/arc-public/state-law-physician-assistant-scope-practice.pdf, accessed June 20, 2021.

50 Interstate Medical Licensure Compact: https://www.imlcc.org/a-faster-pathway-to-physician-licensure/.

51 Karin A. Lips, "California needs to reform nurse licensing requirements," *Los Angeles Daily News,* March 31, 2021, https://www.dailynews.com/2021/03/31/california-needs-to-reform-nurse-licensing-requirements/.

52 California Medical Association Press Release, April 1, 2020, https://www.cmadocs.org/newsroom/news/view/ArticleId/48804/Some-physician-licensing-requirements-waived-during-COVID-19-response.

53 "How the pandemic has impacted policy," Center for Connected Health Policy, https://www.cchpca.org/covid-19-related-state-actions, accessed June 20, 2021.

54   mHealth Intelligence Web site, https://mhealthintelligence.com/news/will-telehealth-payment-parity-be-permanent-or-a-passing-fancy, accessed June 20, 2021.

55   J. Scott Ashwood, Ateev Mehrotra, David Cowling, Lori Uscher-Pines, "Direct-To-Consumer Telehealth May Increase Access To Care But Does Not Decrease Spending," *Health Affairs*, March 2017, https://www.healthaffairs.org/doi/full/10.1377/hlthaff.2016.1130.

56   Centers for Medicare and Medicaid Services, "Hospital Price Transparency," https://www.cms.gov/hospital-price-transparency.

57   Health Care Cost Institute, "Past the Price Index: Exploring the Actual Prices Paid for Specific Services by Metro Area," https://healthcostinstitute.org/in-the-news/hmi-2019-service-prices.

58   Centers for Medicare and Medicaid Services: https://www.cms.gov/newsroom/press-releases/trump-administration-announces-historic-price-transparency-requirements-increase-competition-and, accessed June 20, 2021.

59   Aaron Bloschichak, Anna Milewski, Katie Martin, "CMS-specified shoppable services accounted for 12% of 2017 health care spending among individuals with employer-sponsored insurance," Health Care Cost Institute, Jan. 16, 2020, https://healthcostinstitute.org/hcci-research/cms-specified-shoppable-services-made-up-12-of-2017-health-care-spending-among-people-with-employer-sponsored-insurance-1.

60   Austin Frakt, "How Common Procedures Became 20 Percent Cheaper for Many Californians," *New York Times*, Aug. 8, 2016, https://www.nytimes.com/2016/08/09/upshot/how-common-procedures-got-20-percent-cheaper-for-many-californians.html.

61   Ibid.

62   Ibid.

63   Ibid.

64   Public letter from the Health Policy Consensus Group: https://www.healthcarechoices2020.org/wp-content/uploads/2020/10/2020_08_0206_HealthCareCommentaryPrint_V12.pdf.

ACKNOWLEDGMENTS

I would like to offer a note of gratitude to the contributors to this book. They all are accomplished writers and thinkers who contributed thoughtful chapters because of their desire to improve the state of affairs in California and create a better future for all of us. I'd also like to offer special thanks to Sally Pipes, president of the Pacific Research Institute, for her recognition of the importance of this project and her commitment to make it happen. Thanks also to Dana Beigel, whose fabulous design work always brings sparkle to public-policy topics, and to PRI's Rowena Itchon, Tim Anaya and Evan Harris for their hard work, guidance and support for this book. Despite its criticism of the state's current political trajectory, *Saving California* is a labor of love designed to seek out policy solutions that can once again make this a Golden State that beckons people from around the country and the world.

ABOUT PACIFIC RESEARCH INSTITUTE

The Pacific Research Institute (PRI) champions freedom, opportunity, and personal responsibility by advancing free-market policy solutions. It provides practical solutions for the policy issues that impact the daily lives of all Americans, and demonstrates why the free market is more effective than the government at providing the important results we all seek: good schools, quality health care, a clean environment, and a robust economy.

Founded in 1979 and based in San Francisco, PRI is a non-profit, non-partisan organization supported by private contributions. Its activities include publications, public events, media commentary, community leadership, legislative testimony, and academic outreach.

Center for Business and Economics

PRI shows how the entrepreneurial spirit—the engine of economic growth and opportunity—is stifled by onerous taxes, regulations, and lawsuits. It advances policy reforms that promote a robust economy, consumer choice, and innovation.

Center for Education

PRI works to restore to all parents the basic right to choose the best educational opportunities for their children. Through research and grassroots outreach, PRI promotes parental choice in education, high academic standards, teacher quality, charter schools, and school-finance reform.

Center for the Environment

PRI reveals the dramatic and long-term trend toward a cleaner, healthier environment. It also examines and promotes the essential ingredients for abundant resources and environmental quality: property rights, markets, local action, and private initiative.

Center for Health Care

PRI demonstrates why a single-payer Canadian model would be detrimental to the health care of all Americans. It proposes market-based reforms that would improve affordability, access, quality, and consumer choice.

Center for California Reform

The Center for California Reform seeks to reinvigorate California's entrepreneurial self-reliant traditions. It champions solutions in education, business, and the environment that work to advance prosperity and opportunity for all the state's residents.

Center for Medical Economics and Innovation

The Center for Medical Economics and Innovation aims to educate policymakers, regulators, health care professionals, the media, and the public on the critical role that new technologies play in improving health and accelerating economic growth.

CPSIA information can be obtained
at www.ICGtesting.com
Printed in the USA
BVHW020804230821
615010BV00015B/191